ALEISTER CROWLEY
AND
DION FORTUNE

About the Author

Alan Richardson is the author of more than fifteen books, including magical biographies of Dion Fortune, Christine Hartley, and William G. Gray. He is also an expert on earth mysteries, mythology, Paganism, Celtic lore, and ancient Egypt. Alan does not belong to any occult group or society, does not take pupils, and does not give lectures on any kind of initiation. He insists on holding down a full-time job in the real world like any other mortal. That, after all, is part and parcel of the real magical path. He is married with four children and lives very happily in a small village in the southwest of England. Please visit his website at http://www.alric.pwp .blueyonder.co.uk.

ALEISTER CROWLEY

AND

DION FORTUNE

The Logos of the Aeon and the Shakti of the Age

ALAN RICHARDSON

Llewellyn Publications
Woodbury, Minnesota

First Edition
First Printing, 2009

Book design by Donna Burch
Cover art © Brand X Pictures
Cover design by Kevin R. Brown
Editing by Brett Fechheimer

Llewellyn is a registered trademark of Llewellyn Worldwide, Ltd.

Photo of Aleister Crowley courtesy of William Breeze of the Ordo Templi Orientis (O.T.O.)

Library of Congress Cataloging-in-Publication Data
Richardson, Alan, 1951–
  Aleister Crowley and Dion Fortune : the logos of the Aeon and the
Shakti of the age / Alan Richardson. — 1st ed.
      p. cm.
  Includes bibliographical references.
  ISBN 978-0-7387-1580-3
  1. Crowley, Aleister, 1875–1947. 2. Fortune, Dion. 3. Magicians—England—Biography. 4. Occultists—England—Biography. I. Title.
  BF1598.C7R53 2009
  828'.91209—dc22
  [B]

                                                                            2009030635

Llewellyn Publications
A Division of Llewellyn Worldwide, Ltd.
2143 Wooddale Drive, Dept. 978-0-7387-1580-3
Woodbury, Minnesota 55125-2989, U.S.A.
www.llewellyn.com

Printed in the United States of America

Aleister Crowley

Dion Fortune

Contents

ABOUT THIS BOOK

This is a comparative biography of the two most important magicians of the twentieth century. It will show how they have influenced us all today, whether we realise it or not.

It is not meant as an exhaustive biography so much as a series of essays on patterns. Aleister Crowley and Dion Fortune were bound together by a single beam of light—Magick—and their lives curved, looped, and crossed on either side of this like the twin serpents of the caduceus. Often they mirrored each other, sometimes they conjoined; they always balanced. What I have done is look at that explosion at the top of the caduceus which was so splendidly visible at the end of their lives, and try to track down the central column of magickal light to see where it was rooted in the soil of their birth.

In 1911 Crowley wrote a book called *Liber Thisarb*. Thisarb, he explained, is *Berashith* transliterated backwards—which is the first word of the Bible, meaning 'In the beginning . . . ' In it he showed how to train what he called the Magickal Memory, using a conscious reversal of the order of time, remembering events in reverse sequence like watching a film run backwards. So this present book on both Crowley and Dion Fortune uses the same technique. The biographical and historical details are therefore not given in the usual sequential way, and it tells the story of their lives from their deaths, back toward their births—and beyond. By learning about them in this way the reader will find his or her own mind being stretched as much as informed. The rhythms will startle, and occasionally jolt, but they will also stimulate in ways that any serious student of Magick will recognise and appreciate. By the time it is finished the themes and images will come alive within the readers' psyches, and their own potential for Magickal Memory will be developed to no small degree.

In other words, as Dion Fortune might have said, this book is meant to train the mind as much as inform it.

It is impossible to be objective when writing about any individual. Instead I have tried to be evenhanded. Nevertheless, despite my deep fascination and admiration for many aspects of that phenomenon known as 'Aleister Crowley', my lifelong love affair with 'Dion Fortune' might just incline me toward a certain bias in her direction. There is always the danger of me putting two and two together and making 93. Readers must adjust their own scales of truth and judge me accordingly.

As L. P. Hartley once wrote: 'The past is a foreign country'. So it should be noted that the country we will look at in this book extends not only through time, but in different dimensions, and the inhabitants have customs, attitudes, laws, and ways of thought that might strike us as odd or even repellent today. But it is their country, and they were simply living in their own way, and we should respect that.

Finally, a lot of people have given me a great deal of help in finding obscure facts and information for this project, even though they may not have agreed with my use of the same, or even, it seems, agreed very much with each other: Simon Buxton, Gareth Knight, David Young, William Breeze, Nick Farrell, Maria Babwahsingh, Clive Harper, Jerry Cornelius, Kenneth Grant, Dolores Ashcroft Nowicki, Jo Barnes, R. A. Gilbert, Peter Yorke, and Laura Jennings-

Yorke—plus those others who preferred that I didn't mention their names. Finally, most of all, to my wife, Margaret, and my daughters, Zoe, Kirsty, Jade, and Lara. My thanks to everyone for their patience and kindness.

PROLOGUE

They died within two years of each other: she within the smog-enshrouded Middlesex Hospital, amid the massive bomb damage done to London by six years of war; he in the salt-sea air of Hastings, in a large and stately boarding house with the evocative and curiously apt name of Netherwood.

When the woman died, on 8 January 1946, taken by acute myeloid leukaemia, it had been quite unexpected. She was still young (a mere fifty-five) and had lived a decent life: eating healthy food, taking appropriate exercise in various dimensions, engaging in stimulating mental activity involving august spiritual beings, and she had once written a book about the nature of Purity.

When the man died of a lung infection, on 1 December 1947, unloved in any usual way, no one was at all surprised. In fact they marvelled that he had lasted so long. He was seventy-two, had lived a life of adventure, indecency, and excess; had wrestled with demons of the darkest kind; had been branded by the national press as the Wickedest Man in the World; and finally his drug-wracked body had just given up.

The man's concern, when he got news of her death, was very brief and very cold. He wondered what could be done about her followers.

His own followers were thinning out, and he would have liked to inherit hers. Nothing came of it, however. She passed nothing obvious on to him. In the eyes of history their spirits—which had never seemed particularly close—diverged.

They had never been lovers, it must be said. They had only met in the last few years. In an era when the telephone machine was still something of a rarity, and postal deliveries impressively frequent, their correspondence had been lively but never romantic, or even deep. Almost nothing has survived.

If anything, they were bound by a mutual psychic contact with a non-human being from the very depths of both the human psyche and interstellar space. Had they met when she was a young and fertile priestess and he Pan Ithyphallus he might have tried it on, tried to inflict her with the Serpent's Kiss—biting her lower lip—and thus getting her in his completely amoral power. She might have become his disciple. On the other hand, it is more than likely that she would have shown herself to be far more than he could have coped with, and probably they both knew it.

So they were never lovers in any earthly sense, nor did they work magick in the privacy of his rooms in Hastings; and he would never—not *ever*—have been allowed across the threshold of her own private temples in London and Glastonbury.

Yet, despite that, Aleister Crowley and Dion Fortune produced between them something that was extraordinary, and which has affected us all in the twenty-first century.

They produced an Aeon . . .

chapter one

DEATHS
AND AFTERWARD

If we could have followed their souls after their deaths, we would find them pausing in a place of clear white light that the Eastern Tradition named as *kama loka*, or Plane of Desire. It is a place where each of them would review as if on a cinema screen all that they had done, and were able to decide what adjustments might be made for their next lives on earth. We cannot know what the souls of Aleister Crowley and Dion Fortune saw and felt when they went through this unavoidable process, but we can make our own judgements from the outer details of the lives once lived, and work backwards to the source. This is a case of 'withering into the root', to paraphrase the poet W. B. Yeats—who was no mean magician himself.[1]

The fact is, superficially at least, there can have been few people as different as Aleister Crowley and the woman who used that pen name 'Dion Fortune'. He was known globally by many names and titles, including the Master Therion, Perdurabo, Baphomet, and the Great Beast; she was happy to use her married name of Violet Evans, though she was invariably called just 'Dion' within her narrow circle, or else referred to as DF.

---

1. From the Yeats poem "The Coming of Wisdom with Time" (1910).

The man, as we have noted, was globally regarded as a dark individual who was shot through with brilliance. The woman was seen within her narrow, almost local, circle as someone who shone with light yet who carried bits and pieces of darkness within her. One courted publicity whenever he could. The other shunned it whenever possible. When he died, the news travelled around the world and many people breathed a sigh of relief. After all, he had been pilloried by the international press for decades as 'The Wickedest Man in the World', and there were many who believed this. She on the other hand was known to her limited circle of followers as a true Priestess of the Moon, who died a quiet but radiant death without anyone outside of her circle hearing about her passing or even much caring.

No one knows what Dion's last words were, but the imminence of her demise would not have troubled a woman who had functioned for years as a powerful medium, and who had once written a book called *Through the Gates of Death*. In it she described how the Adept would meet death:

> When the time comes for the adept to set forth, he summons those who are dearest that they may ease his parting and companion him on the first stages of his journey. Those who can come in the flesh gather about; those who cannot, come thither in the astral projection; and those who have gone on ahead through the great Gates are summoned also that they may return and await him upon the threshold.[2]

She had explored the inner planes for most of her life, and so knew what to do and where to go once she had given her last breath. In contrast, Crowley's last words were recorded as either, 'I am perplexed' or 'Sometimes I hate myself'. On the other hand, Deirdre Mac-Alpine, who visited Crowley with their son and found him in light spir-

---

2. Dion Fortune, *Through the Gates of Death* (London: Aquarian Press, 1968), p. 93. First published in 1932.

its and very chatty, reported that there was a sudden gust of wind and peal of thunder at the otherwise quiet moment of his passing, and felt that the Gods were welcoming him home. The great medium Eileen Garrett added, 'Some of the faithful followers who remained with him to the end assured me that his body in death glowed with an intense lustre'.[3]

Crowley's cremation was in Brighton, a large seaside town on the southern coast which has a reputation today as being the gay capital of England. About a dozen people attended, described by one anonymous and rather snobbish observer as comprising 'an odd mixture of crumpled raincoats, coughs, bright scarves, a lack of haircuts and the indefinable spoor of Charlotte Street and Soho'.[4] One of these was his old friend Louis Wilkinson, who read in beautifully modulated tones the 'Hymn To Pan', the 'Collects and Anthems' from The *Gnostic Mass*, and selected passages from the *Book of the Law*. Although he was a self-described poet, it was the 'Hymn to Pan' which was arguably the deceased's most effective piece, with the superb opening lines:

> *Thrill with the lissome lust of the light, O man! My man!*
> *Come careering out of the night*
> *Of Pan! Io Pan!*

This, as you can imagine, was not the most Christian of endings. Shortly after the cremation, a young writer named James Laver mentioned to Wilkinson, 'You know, I would like to write about the life

---

3. Eileen Garrett, *Many Voices: The Autobiography of a Medium* (New York: Putnam, 1968), p. 60.

4. The entire account can be found on the LAShTAL website, at http://www.lashtal .com/nuke/module-subjects-viewpage-pageid-74.phtml (accessed 31 July 2009).

of Crowley now he's safely dead'. Wilkinson slowly faced the young man and asked, 'Ah … but what do you mean by safely dead?'[5]

No details survive of Dion Fortune's funeral, yet despite the overwhelming Pagan tendencies in her final years we might imagine that it would have had strong Christian emphases thanks to the influence of her Jesuit-trained successor Arthur Chichester, whom she thought of as her Sun Priest. As someone who had always wrestled with the androgyny of the human spirit and perhaps within her own self, it was appropriate that she should die in the aptly named Middlesex Hospital, in London. From there her body was driven toward Glastonbury in Somerset, symbolically going 'into the West', as great figures of Celtic and Egyptian mythology were said to do when their lives were ended and missions fulfilled. She was buried in the cemetery which is set on St Edmunds Hill, alongside the Wells Road, within five minutes walk from Glastonbury town centre.

At least Crowley really was, as young James Laver had observed, 'safely dead' this time. Seventeen years before he had actually faked his death, leaving his cigarette case and a hand-written suicide note on the clifftop above the crashing waves at Boca do Inferno (Hell's Mouth), a fearsome ravine that leads to the sea between Sintra and Estoril, near Lisbon. It may have been an attempt to get the many creditors off his back and improve the sales of his books; it may have been part of his long-running efforts for British Intelligence, enabling him to lie low in the nearby resort of Cascais, which was brimming with influential Germans on whom he had a brief to spy; it may simply have been an attempt to escape a discarded lover named Hanni Jaeger. There were rumours in the French press that he had been murdered by assassins from the Vatican. A group of his followers in England held a séance to try and contact his spirit on the other side. Crowley in fact had slipped

---

5. See *Red Flame*, the website of Jerry E. Cornelius, http://www.cornelius93.com/. Information from this website is presented here with the kind permission of Mr Cornelius.

across the border into Spain, where he took great delight in reading the accounts of his suicide in the newspapers.[6]

It might be supposed that Fortune's demise in 1946 was as certain as Crowley's final passing the following year, but one earnest and thoroughly extraordinary person known to me insisted that as a young man he had known her in 1949–50, worked a very different kind of magic with her then, and learned that she had faked her death three years earlier in order to escape the restrictive atmosphere of the group which she had founded. He met her in London, and had liaisons with her in Kewstoke and Uphill in Somerset—small villages next to Weston-super-Mare where she had lived as a young girl. They travelled as aunt and nephew, and their relationship was entirely sexual—though not without fondness. After they parted company because of his imminent marriage, he never saw her again and had no idea when she finally died.

If this astonishing tale is true, then she might have been unconsciously copying Crowley's temporary escape route, which she would have heard about at the time. It must be said, however, that despite this elderly informant's unquestionable sincerity there is absolutely no proof that it really happened. On the other hand there is no proof that it didn't happen either, despite exhaustive enquiries all round. But whether she really died in 1946 or lived on and had adventures and a very different kind of life in the West Country is irrelevant, because the true significance is this:

Just as the myth of Crowley is far more important and potent than the often sordid reality of the man, this account of Dion Fortune existing beyond the accepted date puts her up there with all those Sacred Kings and Queens who never really died but lived on in another way, either in this world or the next. In this respect, the myth of a

---

6. Richard B. Spence, *Secret Agent 666: Aleister Crowley, British Intelligence and the Occult* (Port Townsend, WA: Feral House, 2008), p. 215.

resurrected Dion Fortune is completely relevant and almost necessary, regardless of historical reality.

In fact, the myths of these two have ensured that in some ways they have a more effective existence today than they ever had when in the flesh. Make no mistake . . . Crowley the Magus bore little relationship to Crowley the Man, and it is the former who should inspire us, while the latter provides the 'Terrible Warning' about what not to do. The blending of Violet Evans with the atmosphere of her fictional creation 'The Sea Priestess' gives her shade a power which somehow can influence us from inner levels today.

Aleister Crowley and Dion Fortune may have been—on the surface—very different individuals, but as we will see they were bound together by one thing: they practised High Magic (whichever spelling you prefer) with every fibre of their beings, every moment of every day of their lives. They never compromised, never sold out, and in subtle ways managed to transform the consciousness of generations yet unborn. It was not so much that they were awkward parts in a complicated puzzle that happened to have two bits that would fit, but more a case that they had the elegant curves and harmonies that, for the rest of us, formed a Yin Yang of cosmic significance.

Definitions

So how do we define these titles 'Logos of the Aeon' and 'Shakti of the Age'? What do we mean by this, and how—or why—did they become applied to these two very mortal beings?

Crowley, never one to be modest or mince his words, described himself as a Prophet who was ' . . . chosen to proclaim the Law which will determine the destinies of this planet for an epoch'. In simple terms Christianity had had its day. The Great Beast, as he sometimes styled himself, believed that he heralded another age known as the Aeon of Horus. The mystic 'Word' of this Aeon was Thelema, the Greek word for Will. In Crowley's system it was also related to Agape, the Greek word for Love. The message of Thelema was expressed neatly by the two famous injunctions: 'Do what thou Wilt shall be the whole of the Law'. To which one was supposed to reply, 'Love is the Law; Love under Will'.

He described in his *Confessions* this New Aeon that he had inaugurated, and to him the Aeon of Horus (the Crowned and Conquering Child), while suffering from spasms of transitory passion, would ultimately release mankind from its pretence of altruism, its obsession of fear, and its consciousness of sin. More, it would be seen as utterly conscienceless, cruel, helpless, affectionate, and ambitious. He advised anyone who wanted to understand the Aeon more that many of its characteristics might be found by studying the stigmata of child psychology, concluding: 'And if he possess any capacity for understanding the language of symbolism, he will be staggered by the adequacy and accuracy of the summary of the spirit of the New Aeon given in the *Book of the Law*'.[7]

So an Aeon in Crowley's terms was a period of time ruled by a particular god—in this case Horus. But Gnostic-hearted old soul that he was, he would also have been aware of Valentinus' ideas on the topic.

Valentinus was the most prominent and influential of the historical Christian Gnostics, and seems to have studied with the legendary Basilides in Alexandria, but also received secret teachings from a certain Theodas, allegedly a disciple of St Paul. His system developed a highly complex model of the universe in which each of fifteen successive levels of emanation (Aeons) occurs as a *syzygy*, a male-female pair.

The supreme Divinity was called Bythos (Depth), who is encompassed by Sigê (Silence). Through the interaction of Bythos and Sigê, the first syzygy of Aeons, Nous/Alêtheia, emanated. These gave birth

---

7. *The Confessions of Aleister Crowley*, chapter 49.

to the second syzygy, Logos/Zoê, which brought forth Anthrôpos/ Ekklêsia. And so on.

This can be mind-numbingly complex, but we can put it in a simpler way: from the profound and silent depths of nothingness emerged Intellect and Truth, which created Word and Life (Logos and Zoê), which created Man and Church.

In the Crowleyan sense, if we may use that term, the Logos needed a mate. To him the true partner of the Logos was the Scarlet Woman (of whom more later), but Valentinus with his idea of the syzygy was more right than the Beast: you have to give life to the word, or else it is just noise. Likewise if life is never able to express itself, it is just dead flesh.

So it can be argued that it was Dion Fortune who became the Zoê to Crowley's Logos in the Gnostic magical current channelled by the pair of them.

~

And what is the 'Shakti of the Age' as specifically applied to the vehicle known as Dion Fortune?

This is the great power of Time, creating the different world ages that humanity passes through during the long cycles of cosmic evolution. It is the power of Time that takes humanity from one world age to another, working to sustain the spiritual energy of the planet through the ages of light and darkness. In other words, it was the man who made all the noises, but the woman who made things happen. We can get a glimpse of this in her superb novel *Moon Magic*, in which the great priestess Vivien le Fay Morgan uses her power to free poor Rupert Malcolm, a sexually frustrated and tortured individual, from his lifelong agonies—and in so doing frees humanity also.

Although Miss Morgan's voice was that of the adept Dion Fortune in all her power, the frustrations described—sexual frustrations— were drawn from those of the mortal Violet Firth, as her character thinks of the complete uselessness and wastefulness, the sheer folly of the sacrifice that had been demanded of Dr Malcolm by conventional morality. She thought of the misery, despair, and sheer torture that the conventions and superstitions of mankind had inflicted upon him, and so the great Moon Priestess dealt with it by magical means. In those hours of intense power and emotion within her moon temple, with the great River Thames in flood outside, the magic she did for all men as tortured and agonised as he went into the group mind of the race to work like leaven. 'There is freedom in the world today because of what I did that night, for it opened the first tiny rift in the great barrier and the forces began to move, channelling and eroding as they flowed, till presently the strength of waters came flooding through like the bursting of a dam and all resistance melted away'.[8]

Although this was fiction, there is no doubt that it was based upon some very real magical workings. In their own ways, Aleister Crowley and Dion Fortune broke down barriers for us all.

Unlike Crowley, however, who would happily claim any grandiose title for himself, Dion never saw herself as Shakti of the Age—although she knew that she was just a bit different. Nor did Crowley apply this title to her. In fact she would have abhorred any such description. Yet in 1943 she wrote about the role of her Fraternity:

> We are of the world, but not in it. We cannot be otherwise than a part of our race and age as long as we are inhabiting time and space; yet, mentally, those who accept the viewpoint of the Fraternity, and have been trained in its discipline until that viewpoint guides their lives, are no part of the age in which they live, but of an age that is yet to come.[9]

---

8. Dion Fortune, *Moon Magic: Being the Memoirs of a Mistress of That Art* (York Beach, ME: Red Wheel/Weiser, 2003), pp. 179–80. First published in 1956 by Aquarian Press in London.

9. Dion Fortune (edited by Gareth Knight), *The Magical Battle of Britain* (Bradford on Avon, UK: Golden Gates Press, 1993), p. 104.

She had her own ideas about the forthcoming era. While Crowley may have been hoping that she would use the term Aeon and all that implied, she still preferred to think of it in terms of the Piscean Age giving way to the Aquarian, which in itself was rather a radical concept in that era. In a letter dated 17 January 1944, she wrote to her friend and legal advisor 'HF':

> In the Aquarian Age, or so I believe, there will be a high degree of individualisation combined with a high degree of social integration. This can only be achieved if each individual has a strong sense of social duty; if each citizen says in the true sense, 'L'etat, c'est moi'. We can judge the rightness or wrongness of any action by extending it in a straight line and asking ourselves what would happen if everyone did that? . . . Now I believe that evolution is pioneered by those individuals who have the knowledge living according to the principles of the new age. I and my group try to live as Aquarians . . . [10]

She went on to insist that while there are certain standards which are eternal, such as truth and honesty, there are others that change with the changing age: the qualities that make a man a good citizen in wartime may make him a gangster in peace; while the qualities that make a good citizen in peace time could well make the wretch a brake on the wheel during warfare. Perhaps with one eye on the example of the dark lord himself, Crowley, she noted that different conditions make different demands, and the qualities that constitute good citizenship change with the changing times.

Just as one never realises an Age has passed until it is long gone, it is only in retrospect that we can see what she embodied. In the years after her passing, when people have had a chance to assess her impact, more and more have come to think of her as someone who brought through the great energies of change and transformation

---

10. From the personal collection of Maria Babwahsingh, with the kind permission of Ms. Babwahsingh.

that we have experienced since. But whereas the Master Therion thundered out 'Do what Thou Wilt' as a prerequisite for illumination, Dion Fortune insisted that every one of her initiates had to be able to say: 'I desire to Know, in order to Serve'.

⌒

But what do we mean by Magic, as she termed it, and Magick, as Crowley preferred?

He defined magick with a 'k' as 'the Science and Art of causing Change to occur in conformity with Will'. He also said: '. . . every intentional act is a Magickal Act'. He preferred the terminal 'k' because it distinguished the ancient art from mere conjuring. Plus the 'k' signified to him the 'kteis', or vagina, and hinted at the sexual nature of his own expressed Mysteries.

Without endorsing the sexual interpretation implied by the final 'k', Dion Fortune slightly modified this by adding a couple of words: 'changes in consciousness', so that her own definition became: 'Magic is the art of causing changes to occur in consciousness, in conformity with will'.

To both of them, changing consciousness and tuning it towards higher levels of awareness—towards the very Gods themselves—was a near-forgotten part of human evolution, and a religious quest of the most holy kind.

Legacies

When they died, what legacies did they leave?

In material terms, it can be seen that Crowley had over the years squandered every penny of his originally huge inheritance and had a mere £18 left. Dion, however, had used her own accrued wealth so carefully that she had £9,781 in her account.

On another level the man left behind him a legacy of two organisations, known as the A. A. and the O. T. O.

The former was founded in 1906 by himself and George Cecil Jones. Crowley never explained what A. A. stands for, and the versions are invariably . . . Argenteum Astrum, Argentinum Astrum (both meaning Silver Star), but plausibly also Arcanum Arcanorum (Secret of Secrets), or absurdly, Atlantean Adepts. Gerald Yorke, who was a member, described the A. A. as Rosicrucianism with the sex put back. Crowley himself defined the A. A. as ' . . . the one true and invisible Order which has operated under various names and guises throughout history to guide the spiritual evolution of humanity. The goals of the A. A. are those which have motivated spiritual exploration and religious inquiry throughout human history. Its methods are those of science; its aims are those of religion'.

The second organisation, the Ordo Templi Orientis, was probably founded in Germany around 1895, but Crowley assumed the title of Outer Head of the Order in 1925. Although originally structured along Freemasonic lines, he re-created it as a vehicle for expressing the Law of Thelema, and it still exists today although there are many—frequently antagonistic—variations.

In comparison, Dion Fortune founded her Fraternity of the Inner Light in 1922 as an offshoot—like the A. A.—from the legendary Hermetic Order of the Golden Dawn, using a system of training and progressive initiation leading to individual gnosis. If Crowley very often had to operate his rites from a variety of apartments or basements (or as it was rumoured on at least one occasion in Paris, breaking into a church and using a naked woman on her hands and knees as an altar), she had two substantial temples in London and a smaller one in Glastonbury from which to operate. The FIL still exists today as the Society of the Inner Light, nearly a century after it was created.

In some ways they functioned within the collective unconscious like the spheres of Chockmah and Binah on the kabbalistic Tree of Life which we will look at later, and which Dion and Crowley interpreted so profoundly many decades before modern celebrities with more money than sense started making such a fuss about their own vapid versions, and wearing those ridiculous red bracelets.

But on yet another and far more effective level their crucial legacies are to be found in those subtle but immensely potent myths and legends which came to surround them, and which have stimulated the psyches and awakened the inner senses of countless seekers since. As already mentioned, the myth and legend of a person invariably has far greater power and endurance than the reality, and we have to look at these as the legacies meant for us.

Crowley in his time had been a world-class mountaineer and conquered some of the highest peaks in the Himalayas; there are climbers today who hero-worship him for those feats alone and have no time for the magickal side. He was a chess master (although some said he used hypnotic techniques to beat his opponents), highly regarded (especially by himself) as a poet, explorer, hunter, trickster, bully, secret agent, novelist, socialite, sponger, libertine, heroin addict, and writer of some of the most influential occult books of the twentieth century. After 1904, when he had a cosmic revelation in Cairo, he devoted the rest of his life to what he called *Crowleyanity*.

He was a true eccentric, an underground hero, a dark utopian, a recognisable forerunner of the sex and drugs and rock 'n' rollers nearly three generations before rock music appeared; and he was eventually adored by the gods of rock when they discovered him: the Beatles, the Rolling Stones, David Bowie, Ozzy Osbourne and Black Sabbath, Iron Maiden, and Jimmy Page of Led Zeppelin to name but a few, and later on numerous punk bands also took him on board, recognising the outrageous rebel in him.

For decades you couldn't open a novel without a thinly disguised version of him appearing as a veritable Prince of Darkness,[11] and appearing in more memoirs than probably anyone else simply be-cause—love or loathe him—you could never quite forget him. In some ways he can seem worse to us today than ever because of his open use and espousal of drugs such as cocaine, opium, laudanum, and mescaline, but in his youth these were entirely legal substances. The saddest thing was that he might have been a god incarnate, or at very least a vehicle for such, but he never kicked his heroin addic-tion, despite all his efforts over many years.

In literary terms Crowley's own books, most of which he self-published, hardly attracted many readers in his lifetime, but his ex-traordinary *Confessions* has never been out of print in forty years and exists on the World Wide Web in various electronic forms, hovering in cyberspace like the ka of some mummified Egyptian priest.

To his critics at the time (i.e., almost everyone on the planet), the philosophy of Thelema was one of devil worship and what they charmingly termed 'sexual deviancy', for he was as openly bisexual as anyone dared to be then. Young people of today, taking their cur-rent sexual freedoms for granted, don't realise how many of these were made possible because he took that first step forward in moral-ity, which seemed at the time to be so deeply immoral. The world hated him so much that you had to have a sneaking admiration for his sheer guts. The Wickedest Man in the World, as the papers called him, was also in many ways the bravest.

And then there was Dion Fortune. What did she leave us?

Whatever Crowley did for magick from the masculine point of view, DF, as they called her, did very quietly and secretly from the

11. See Martin Booth, *A Magick Life: The Life of Aleister Crowley* (London: Hodder & Stoughton), 2000.

distaff side. Also, like Crowley, an initiate in the Hermetic Order of the Golden Dawn, her own fraternity worked the magic of the West: of Atlantis, Ys, and Egypt; of the Celts and Scandinavians; of King Arthur and the Holy Grail. She made the Kabbalah accessible and lucid, took mediumship to new heights, and explored all of those obscure by-ways that might now be termed 'Native British'—and made them international.

Although there was a Christian Mystic section within her lodge for the less able, she specialised in working with the Great Goddess figures, and toward the end of her life was at times completely overshadowed by these. Her books such as *The Mystical Qabalah*, *Applied Magic*, and the very odd *Psychic Self-Defence* have been much copied but never surpassed. Her novels *The Sea Priestess* and *Moon Magic* are utterly beautiful in their prose and almost hypnotic in their magical effect upon the reader. One critic at the time threw *Moon Magic* aside in utter disgust when the female character said to the sexually frustrated man: 'What you really want to know is exactly how far I go . . .' No one would turn a hair if a woman today spoke like that, but in the 1930s this was very strong and dangerous stuff indeed. People born after the 1960s often don't realise how odd, weird, and radical the notion of Goddess worship and sexually confident women seemed in the years, decades, and even centuries before that. These burgeoning notions were seen then as radical, highly risible, and possibly even dangerous. Thanks to the magical work that DF did within the Collective Unconscious, women today have voices and choices that were unknown to her own parents' generation.

Every woman since who has ever challenged the patriarchy of modern times should give her no small degree of gratitude for paving the way, and showing that—starting on the inner planes—it is Woman who has the power. Quite simply, Dion Fortune brought the Goddess back into the world.

Every modern magician of either sex, meanwhile, owes her a debt for the sheer clarity of exposition on obscure Hermetic topics they might never have grasped otherwise. When you see the present upsurge of interest in ley-lines and earth energies, of seasonal rituals, Old Gods and Older Goddesses, and all things purely Western—including her own interpretation of the Kabbalah seventy years before it became an empty cult—then so very much of it can be tracked back directly to her influence.

And *then* there were the witches.

Where did Crowley and Fortune stand in regard to them?

At the time of this writing, Wicca is regarded in some quarters as the fastest-growing religion in the world. It is a belief system and way of life based upon the reconstruction of pre-Christian traditions, with its spiritual roots in the earliest expressions of reverence for nature, and for both the Goddess and God. It accepts reincarnation and the reality of magick, ritual observance of astronomical and agricultural phenomena, and the use of magickal circles for ritual purposes. And it has long been believed that one of the founders of the movement, Gerald Brosseau Gardner, received much of his Craft material from Crowley.

Despite the stories it has proved difficult to find hard evidence of an actual collaboration between Crowley and Gardner on Wicca, although it is true that Crowley sold him a charter for £300 to run a lodge of the O. T. O. In his Magical Diary for 1947 he makes four brief references to GBG between 1 and 27 May, but nothing before or beyond that.

Nevertheless, Gardner's writings from 1949 onward show that large sections of the Wiccan 1st–3rd Degree Initiations and the Sabbat Rituals are taken word for word from the *Book of the Law* and the

Gnostic Mass.[12] Jerry E. Cornelius has identified those numerous parts of the Gardnerian system which were taken directly from Crowley's existing books, and these are given in appendix A, in order to show which of the Great Beast's concerns were of particular interest to Gardner.

Understand that Crowley did not write these at Gardner's request: Gardner simply lifted almost word for word what he wanted from books by AC that were already in print. So it can be seen that AC did not write rituals for Gardner—who was more than capable of doing so himself. In fact it might said that a magician (or witch) who can't write his or her own rituals shouldn't really be in the business in the first place. Nor is there any truth in the rumour—more of a legend by now—that Crowley had once joined a witch coven but didn't like being bossed about by women. That was never more than a simple English 'fib', a joke, that escaped into the larger world and expanded to fit.

In actual fact Crowley had long had a certain sympathy for the sort of worship that Gardner came to create, as he once expressed in a letter to Charles Stansfield Jones, long before the former came on the scene:

> The time is just ripe for a natural religion. People like rites and ceremonies, and they are tired of hypothetical gods. Insist on the real benefits of the Sun, the Mother-force, the Father-force and so on; and show that by celebrating these benefits worthily the worshippers unite themselves more fully with the current of life . . . [13]

---

12. See, particularly, *Red Flame*, http://www.cornelius93.com/, for Jerry Cornelius' detailed comparison.

13. Quoted in John Symonds, *The Great Beast* (London: Mayflower, 1973).

By the same token a number of researchers have tried hard to find links between Dion Fortune and the Wiccan movement, without any success. Although in the years immediately after her death the Society of the Inner Light had a chalet called 'Avalon' in one of the two nudist camps at Bricket Wood—where Gardner performed what might be thought of as Dionysian rites—DF was never part of this in her lifetime. Also, it seems unlikely that her followers indulged after she had gone.

What the Wiccans got from Dion Fortune was a *tone*. And they got this through her writings, and/or perhaps from her actual spirit. In one of her earliest short stories she described how certain rituals can set off on a note on the inner planes that people attuned to the magic can hear, and be drawn toward. We can hear this ourselves in her two finest novels *The Sea Priestess* and its sequel *Moon Magic*, which she hoped would have self-initiatory qualities—which they did, and do. There is a rhythm in the prose which is utterly compelling, and a power in the imagery which almost effects a very real kind of 'initiation' in the truest sense: a beginning. An awakening. And what the reader hears is the whispering of the Goddess saying, *I'm here. Come work with me* . . .

In fact, both novels contain enough details and teaching for anyone with no previous knowledge of magic whatsoever to construct their own rituals, and get results. And this is what the early postwar Wiccans did. As many modern researchers have shown time and again, the various founders of Wicca sought to gain some validity for their new religion by claiming (spurious) heritages of ancient covens which passed down their secrets through the centuries. This is hardly a crime: the founders of the Hermetic Order of the Golden Dawn did much the same thing seventy years before with the forged documents they claimed—for a time—gave them legitimacy. Nineteen hundred years before *that*, St Paul did similar when he created Christianity.

Once again we are in the realm of 'fibbing', which might be defined as telling harmless and even charming lies, usually with a jokey basis, and often to impose a point of view against all the odds. In this respect, one of the Stately Crones of England (a self-styled 'hereditary witch' of real power and vision) once confessed to me that she had made it all up. And both of us knew that it didn't matter one bit. As Gardner might have said, paraphrasing Crowley: An it harm none, do what ye will.

In reality the Wiccans plundered Robert Graves' *White Goddess* and James Frazier's *Golden Bough* for details of their deities or even coven names, but when it came to fine-tuning their rituals it was the works of Crowley and Fortune that provided them with their rationale, energy, and direction.

And the crucial fact to understand is that, as with the impressive adeptii of the Golden Dawn, they got their system to work.

Fortune's last two novels alone are filled with chants, invocations, Words of Power, and above all those curiously seductive prose rhythms which make the imagery sink deep into the reader's psyche. And while this was written up as fiction, every word was drawn from her own personal experience.

> There was nothing of the human left about me. I was vast as the universe; my head among the stars; my feet on the curve of the earth as it swung under me in its orbit. Around me, in translucent space, stood the stars, rank upon rank, and I was of their company. Beneath me, very far beneath me, all Nature lay spread like a green-patterned carpet. Along on the globe that soared through space I stood . . . [14]

And also, referring to the priest she was working with:

---

14. *Moon Magic*, p. 146.

I was his anima, his underworld contact, his link with most ancient earth and things primordial wherein are the roots of strength;
through me he could touch them as he was powerless to do alone,
for man is of the sun and stars and fire; but woman is of dark space
and dark earth and dark, primordial water . . . [15]

Because of the work those two did on the inner planes, which eventually worked through the Collective Unconscious and found results
in the outer world, young women would never again be committed to
asylums or workhouses for the dreadful sin of getting pregnant outside
of marriage; children would never again be stigmatised by the term
'bastard'; gay men and women would no longer be seen as committing
crimes against humanity; and sexual desire became recognised as a
normal impulse, and not a degradation. It was not so much, *Do* what
thou wilt, but a case of learning to *Be* what you were inside, under the
freedom and challenge of Love.

Toward the end of her life Dion Fortune apparently had a lot of
problems with being so overshadowed by these Goddess archetypes.
Crowley the Man, in contrast, became too frail to fully channel the
Great Gods of Pan and Horus that had once been so omnipresent.

Then again you can forgive them for flagging at the ends of their
extraordinary lives, because they had both come through a terrible
war . . .

---

15. *Moon Magic*, p. 147.

chapter two

THE WARS
OF THEIR WORLDS

The first bombs were dropped by the Luftwaffe on London on 24 August 1940, and the Blitz itself started on 7 September. In the following three-month period alone, 44,717 men, women, and children had been killed in bombing raids and many more than that injured. By the time the Nazis had been defeated, a total of 60,585 British civilians had been killed and another 86,175 seriously wounded by German air raids and the pilotless flying bombs known as the V-1 and supersonic V-2, which no one could hear coming.

London at that time was not exactly a healthy place to be. Some fled overseas. Others took up residence in the countryside. Crowley and Fortune stayed put as long as they could, with a bloody-minded determination to see it through. Although they were too old for active service, the Beast and Mrs Evans were, in their own quite separate ways, anxious to 'do their bit' as they said then, and make sure that this upstart Adolf Hitler was defeated. They both understood that spirituality and pacifism are not necessarily synonymous—at least not when the future of humanity was at stake.

To many at the time this was almost a Holy War, a battle of Light and Darkness, the latter manifesting through the phenomenon of Nazism that is still seen as unquestionably and genuinely evil today, generations afterward. What better could they do than bring all their magic and magick to bear, as best they could, upon the enemy?

If they were joined together by their passion for Magic, they were equally bound by their innate patriotism, and although Crowley had once been branded a traitor twenty years before it is certain now that—as he had said all along—he had been effectively used as a double agent by British Intelligence for many years.[1] At the very least he claimed to have provided Winston Churchill (to whom he bore a startling resemblance) with the iconic two-fingered V for Victory sign, which he insisted represented Apophis (the ancient spirit of destruction) and Typhon (the storm-bringer).

And if they were fighting the Nazis on both outer and inner levels, as we will see, they—Dion in particular—were also fighting wars within their own souls, to try to bring some peace and balance there also.

Before we look at the separate work they did in the Second World War, what actual contact did Crowley and Fortune have at this or indeed any other time? Despite rumours it is highly unlikely that they ever had sex. Crowley, who mentioned just about everything else in his Magical Diaries, would certainly have told us if he had tupped the redoubtable Sea Priestess, and probably given us a detailed description of her yoni as well.

However we do find the following, and this is the first reference to her, dated 12 July 1937:

> Symbol for W-K & the Dion Fortune affair . . . Bought shirt, stockings, tie. Wrote important letters: re. I *Ching* book. Dion Fortune.[2]

---

1. See Richard B. Spence, *Secret Agent 666*.

2. All entries from AC's diaries, and letters from DF to AC, are courtesy of the Ordo Templi Orientis archives, by kind permission of William Breeze.

W-K may be someone named West-Kelsey, although it is quite possibly a reference to W. K. Creasy, a senior figure within the Fraternity of the Light whose wife publicly accused him of having an affair with its founder. No one (except the wounded party) would worry too much about that sort of accusation today, but in 1937 it was explosive. This was not the first time Dion had had this accusation levelled at her: Mrs Zoe Seymour also accused Dion of having an affair with her husband Lt Colonel Charles 'Kim' Seymour, who in some areas was the dominant male magician within the lodge, plus its best scholar and writer. And on top of that a certain Mrs Loveday spent the rest of her life blaming Dion for breaking up her marriage to Charles Thomas Loveday, DF's earliest supporter and champion of the Christian Mystical aspects within her lodge.

Whether there was any substance to these accusations, it's apparent that, in the eyes of those troubled wives at least, Dion Fortune was the very incarnation of a Scarlet Woman. And if anyone could advise her about such tricksy marital fall-outs then it was Crowley, for his whole life had revolved around such happenings.

Is there any value in such gossip? Yes. Yes, there is. Because when Edward Alexander Crowley and Violet Mary Firth, to give them their birth names, became Aleister Crowley and Dion Fortune they entered the realms of myth and legend. When this happens, then every small morsel of existing rumour becomes material for the mythological process. Just as folklorists today pounce upon anything that might emerge having to do with figures such as Merlin, King Arthur, Boudicca, Rolling Thunder, or even John F. Kennedy, then in centuries to come (if the world still survives) all of this about Dion Fortune will have been elevated from the level of mere gossip into that of pure folklore.

Whoever he was, W-K sends Crowley a letter on 10 July and the two of them meet at El Vino, the restaurant in Fleet Street, London, although he tells us nothing more about that.

Later the same year, on 25 November 1937, Crowley notes, 'David Wood—Dion F's gang. Might be good man if taught'.

Later still, in his 1939 diaries he mentions, 'Mr & Mrs Evans for Chili con'. And that same evening he adds in his diary, 'Lawrence Evans calls for me. Dion Fortune—Public Bat No 1 at The Belfry. Like a hippo with false teeth. Talk—bubbling of tinned tomato soup'.

Lawrence Evans is unknown, but the Mr Evans is of course husband of the woman known as Dion Fortune. Known to his intimates as Merl (short for Merlin), Dr Thomas Penry Evans was a deeply psychic though at that time deeply troubled man, regarded by those he allowed close as one of the truly high-powered magicians within her fraternity, and devoted not only to High Magic but to all aspects of healing.

Despite AC's cruel comment about bats, the reference to the Belfry is to the temple she created on West Halkin Street which was devoted to the Rites of Isis. Alan Adams, a pukka occultist who later formed his own group and wrote about DF under the name 'Charles Fielding', outlined the memories of someone who had been present when the pair met briefly: 'Dion Fortune entered the room [in The Belfry] with some of her friends to find Crowley already seated there in company with two of his scarlet women. He got up (an uncharacteristic gesture) and bowed to her. She replied with a curt British bow and passed on to her seat. That seemed to have been the beginning of a mutual acknowledgement. Subsequently, they exchanged a number of letters and Crowley called her his Moon Priestess, apparently believing that she epitomised the role'.[3]

There has been a simplistic tendency among British occultists in particular to regard Aleister Crowley and Dion Fortune as Black

---

3. Charles Fielding and Carr Collins, *The Story of Dion Fortune* (Loughborough, UK: Thoth Publications, 1998).

and White Magicians respectively, which is an attitude that shows no understanding whatsoever of Magick itself, or these two individual practitioners. There has also been an attempt to minimise or even deny any meaningful contact between them, and passionate fans of DF can get quite twitchy about this. However, she sent him a nice letter on 8 January 1942, which reads in full:

> Dear 666,
> Many thanks for your letter and card. I am glad you find my taber-nacles pleasant. I saw designs for two of your Tarot trumps at the Atlantis Book shop when calling upon Michael Juste, and thought them very fine. I should be interested to know when they are pub-lished. I have, I think, most of your books, but not 'Thumbs Up'.
>
> I am afraid my Biblical Knowledge has grown rusty and I can-not follow the reference to Daniel and the Apocalypse with regard to Mr. Churchill, so you will have to dot the I's if you want to con-vey anything to my intelligence, which you over-estimate. Is Mr. Churchill to be conceived of as crowned with the stars, or does his tail draw the twelfth part of them after him?
>
> My mentality always has hampered my work, and, I am afraid, always will.
>
> With all good wishes for the success of your Tarot, which cer-tainly deserves it.
>
> > Yours sincerely,
> > Dion Fortune

The next entry in Crowley's diaries is dated 12 January 1942, when he writes, 'Letter from Dion Fortune, Replied, sending her T. U.! Both editions'.

T. U. refers to the fourteen-page pamphlet 'THUMBS UP: A Pen-tagram—a Panticle to Win the War', which Crowley released in two versions in 1941. One 'Privately Published in London', and the other 'Privately Published in New York'.

Kenneth Grant, the head of the Typhonian O. T. O. and a personal pupil of Crowley, told me in a letter that DF and AC had had quite an extensive correspondence, though nothing of any real depth was touched upon, and the vast bulk has disappeared to America, or been destroyed. It has to be remembered that in those times telephones were not universal, and letters were the medium of choice. With four postal deliveries a day, it would have been possible for Crowley to send Dion a letter at breakfast and receive a reply by lunchtime—or tea-time, at the latest. The fact that there was an extensive and cordial correspondence between them is not in itself significant, however, but it shows that she herself—with her formidable psychic perceptions—did not write him off as 'Black'.

In 1944 Crowley published the *Book of Thoth* with its sublime tarot designs, and one of the subscribers was Dion Fortune. When he sent her a copy of the book he inscribed it fulsomely: 'To Dion Fortune, this small tribute to her achievement and attainment in the Science of Wisdom and to her eminence as an Artist in Words. No. 9 to Dion Fortune, as to the High Priestess of Our Lady Selene. "The number 9 is sacred, and attains the summit of philosophy". Zoroaster'.

He also sent her two extraordinary paintings that had originally been given to him by J. F. C. Fuller, entitled 'The Portal of the Outer Order' and the 'Portal of the Second Order'. Again, her acceptance of these is no evidence of anything other than politeness. But she kept them, and she didn't destroy them as being tainted in any way.

Then there is an entry in Crowley's diary for 1 January 1945: 'Dion Fortune sent a Qy. And £5.5.0 for Ans. And 3 letters!' Presumably she had asked his advice on certain matters. She might have been a great magician, mediating spiritual forces, but sometimes she could also be Violet Evans (née Firth), who could be as lost and lonely and confused as the rest of us—Crowley included. It is also quite likely that she sought to help him out a little financially by doing this, because that was a decent sum of money in those days.

Then on 8 February of that same year he notes: 'Sent M[inutum] M[undum] to Dion Fortune', which was presumably a diagram of the Tree of Life showing the Paths and connecting Spheres in their appropriate colours, although she would have been more than aware of this diagram, as she had used it in her own classic book on the topic. However if some people in Olde England were mystically and emotionally joined at subtle levels by old school ties and memories of things past and lost from their youths, this pair were joined by the glyph of the kabbalistic *otz chaim*, or Tree of Life.

The next mention does not appear in print until the spring of 1946, by which time she was already dead. It lists her among all those who received the Word of the Equinox. This took the form of a letter, always on one sheet, giving a 'word' and I Ching hexagram to govern the coming six months, sometimes with commentary. It was sent out every spring and autumn. The intriguing thing is this was sent to all those who were deemed as part of Crowley's immediate circle.

Saturnus = Karl Germer
J. W. P. = John Whiteside Parsons
L. U. W. = Louis Umfraville Wilkinson
H. A. = Grady McMurtry
V. I. = Gerald Yorke
E. N. F. = Edward Noel Fitzgerald
R. Cecil = Robert Cecil
B. Crow
G. K. Grant
D. Curwen
F. Mellinger
J. G. Bayley
Ethel Archer
Alexander Watt
Dion Fortune
Tranchell Hayes

Estai 516 = Jane Wolfe

Lady Aberconway

Lady Freida Harris

Of these, nine were O. T. O. members: Germer, Parsons, Wilkinson, McMurtry, Fitzgerald, Curwen, Mellinger, Wolfe, and Harris—one in New York, one (from California) in Germany, three in California, and three in England (not counting Crowley). Crowley had Jane Wolfe recopy the Word for redistribution to the other members in California.

And then there was Dion Fortune. What was the significance of her being on the mailing list? Does this mean that she was, in some covert sense, a member of the A. A.? Or was Crowley recognising her status as Magister Templi (a title we will look at later)?

The G. K. Grant mentioned in the list above was Kenneth Grant, also known by his Magical Name as Aossic. Seen by many (though not all) as the present-day head of the O. T. O., and something of a successor to Crowley himself, Grant's own memories of having been present at several meetings between DF and AC are worth summarising:

> I met her in 1945. She was close to death and had lost much of the physical force and vigour that is so apparent in the photograph . . . . Even so, she conveyed (*transmitted*, would be a better word) a tremendous psychic vitality which struck me very forcibly at the time . . . It was obvious to me then, and the conviction grows stronger each time I read anything by her, that Dion saw herself as *the* magical shakti of the new Aeon . . . I remember her zest in discussing with Aleister the possibility of reviving the Pagan attitudes to cosmic and elemental forces.[4]

In a letter to me dated 17 October 1987, he also recalled another meeting:

---

4. Letter to Janine Chapman dated 9 August 1973. Quoted in Janine Champan, *The Quest for Dion Fortune* (York Beach, ME: Weiser, 1993).

D. F. came to consult A. C. about some ritual or other which involved the sacrifice of a cock. The conversation veered to transhu-
man Intelligence, and D. F. spoke about an entity every bit as awesome as Aiwass. Unfortunately I do not recall the name . . .

She sent the Beast a copy of *The Sea Priestess* in June 1944, and on
14 March 1945, had written to him:

> The acknowledgement I made in the introduction to *The Mystical
> Qabalah* of my indebtedness to your work, which seemed to me
> no more than common literary honesty, has been used as a rod for
> my back by people who look on you as Antichrist. I am prepared
> to dig in my toes and stand up to trouble if I have got to, but I don't
> take on a fight if I can help it nowadays because it wastes too much
> time. I am fully aware that there will come a time when I shall
> have to come out into the open and say: This is the law of the New
> Aeon, but I want to pick my time for that, because I propose to
> be in a strong strategic position when I do so, and if you give Mrs
> Grundy advance information, I may not be properly entrenched
> when the inevitable blitz starts. Therefore I ask you not to mention
> my name for the present. Am at work on a book on the paths . . . .[5]

Casual readers will flash past that paragraph without a second
thought; others, with perhaps a vested interest in an 'approved' interpretation of Dion Fortune, will be brought up in their tracks, for this
is like an Anglican being told that the staid and stiff Archbishop of
Canterbury is really a writhing tantric sex-beast from the Mauve Zone.
It could be read as an indication that she was ready to announce her
acceptance of Thelema—the Law—when times were right.

Those who have that vested interest in a 'correct' version of Dion
Fortune, i.e., one without any Crowleyan overtones or undertones,
have cast doubts on the veracity of this letter. Personally I have no
doubt that it is genuine, for it is written in the everyday and quite

---

5. Kenneth Grant, *Remembering Aleister Crowley* (London: Skoob, 1991).

marked style of Mrs Evans, and it would need a literary genius to be able to mimic that. As will be seen, there are indications that AC and DF really did have a certain 'secret agreement' of sorts.

It is quite possible that DF, while agreeing with the notion in the broadest sense, resisted Crowley's pressure to declaim the Law of Thelema because her own take on the matter was very different to his, and because she just knew that most of her followers—some of whom were still very much attached to the outer court represented by her Guild of the Master Jesus—could never have made the leap.

In fact, the four simple words *Do What Thou Wilt*, which form the crux of what some have termed Crowleyanity, are amenable to such a wide variety of interpretation that people at opposite ends of the magickal spectrum can feel absolutely certain that their very different practices and lifestyles are exemplified by the same axiom. Its meaning can change depending upon which word you emphasise. William G. Gray, the innovative kabbalist and abrasive Adept who had sat on Crowley's lap as a boy, once told me that the crucial word is *Thou*. He would utter it: 'Do what *Thou* wilt'. To him, this referred to the innermost spirit, and so it was an injunction to express the evolutionary drive of the Higher Self rather than the involutionary whims and libidinous impulses of the grossest ego.

It was plain, however, from DF's references to trenches and blitzes, that things in the outer world were far more pressing. The truth is, they both had far more important things to be doing in those six years of the war than fiddling about with doctrine and groups. First they had to survive, and then they had to come out fighting, bringing all the Gods and Goddesses they could summon.

⁓

If braver souls ventured out to watch the battle in the skies above them, they would see the squadrons of Dornier and Heinkel bombers, the bent-wing Stukas with their dreadful sirens, being ripped into by the vastly outnumbered Spitfires and Hurricanes. While on the inner planes, much the same sort of combat was going on.

As is well documented by now, there really was an 'occult' aspect to the Third Reich, although there is also fierce debate as to how much Adolf Hitler himself was directly involved. Two popes, Pius XII and Benedict XVI, spoke about a demonic possession of Hitler (who in 1939 had been nominated for the Nobel Peace Prize!), and Pope Pius even performed an exorcism on the Führer at a distance, but failed.

There is no doubt, however, that Heinrich Himmler, one of his deputies, was as deeply into magic as anyone could be. In some ways he would be seen today as a typical New Age type: into herbalism, astrology, 'earth consciousness', ergonomics, sound natural farming techniques in agriculture, sustainable energy, plus a keen love of animals and children. Yet he created one of the most ruthless organisations of all time and sought to exterminate an entire race. In 1929 Himmler took control of Hitler's small group of personal bodyguards known as the *Schutzstaffel*, or SS, and expanded it hugely within the next few years, establishing its headquarters at a medieval castle called Wewelsburg, where his secret inner order met once a year.

His order—for that was how he thought of it now—owed a certain debt to the legend of King Arthur and the Knights of the Round Table. The great dining hall was adorned with the coats of the arms of the twelve senior *Gruppenführers*, who gathered around a huge oak table, each in his own chair with an engraved silver nameplate, each following a routine of spiritual exercises. Underneath this hall was a 'realm of the dead', a well in which these coats of arms would be burnt and the ashes worshipped after the 'knight' had died. There are tales of Himmler using the severed heads of deceased SS officers to communicate with his ascended masters, and he was said to converse with the ghost of the Saxon king Henry the Fowler.

And each one of these Nazi knights, it must be emphasised, earnestly believed that he was working for the Light, fighting against the Black Magicians which assailed them at all quarters.

There was nothing like Wewelsburg in Britain. At least not on the outer planes. Which didn't mean that the British were sitting back and taking it, passively hoping for some Higher Powers to make it all come good. In fact, the British magicians rolled up their sleeves, took up their wands, and in their own quiet ways proceeded to give the Nazis a hammering . . .

In his long essay entitled 'The Occult Secret Service',[6] Michael Howard has shown how His Majesty's Government was able to draw upon a surprising variety of individuals when it came to launching magical attacks upon the nation's enemies:

> Allegedly SOE [Special Operations Executive] also had an ultra-secret occult research section and psychops unit codenamed Project Seven (P7). This was run by . . . Commander Denton Soames RN, and his agents used such esoteric codenames as 'Archangel', 'Seraphim' and 'Merlin'. It is possible that P7 was behind the story that during the Blitz psychics used telepathic powers to deflect German bomber pilots into ambushes with RAF Spitfires.

In fact, it seems that one of their most successful operatives, a female codenamed 'Anne', used her talent for astral projection to spy on the German High Command. There are even rumours that the Secret Service made use of the psychic powers of the witch covens in the Costwolds to fight the Nazis.

Actually, this now seems less bizarre as details of the American CIA-funded projects of the 1970s—Sun Streak and Grill Flame—emerge: these projects used psychics in exactly the same way against

6. *The Cauldron* (London), issue no. 126, November 2007.

the Russians, and had some extraordinary results with their 'remote viewing' techniques, not to mention their attempts to influence the minds of Russian individuals.[7]

Christine Hartley, who at one time had been something of an heir apparent to Dion Fortune, told me a lot about her experiences fighting the Nazis on the inner planes on a one-to-one basis, going 'into the crystal' and seeking out those foes threatening Britain on magical levels. Interestingly she said that she could cope with the German magicians, but she had had real trouble with the man who lay *behind* Hitler on the inner planes, naming him as the Grand Mufti of Jerusalem, Al-Hajj Amin al-Husayni, who had once written personally to Hitler from Baghdad requesting German assistance in overthrowing the British in Iraq. The mindset of this man, she said, was so alien to anything she had yet encountered, and was so personally inimical to things Western—especially British—that she sometimes feared for more than her life. He probably spoke very highly of her, too.

Meanwhile, Dion Fortune herself organised her group into practicing a series of regular meditations intended to contact the group mind of the nation and bring through the necessary energies. She was certain that there was an active centre of spiritual influence on the inner planes that was broadcasting telepathically certain spiritual ideals. On the other hand she was quite certain that something of the opposite was going on, too:

> We are, in my opinion, dealing with definite occult forces being used telepathically on the group souls of nations, and finding expression through the subconsciousness of susceptible people who lack spiritual principles. I am satisfied that we are not the only group that is broadcasting to the subconscious mind of the race; and that just as we have found ourselves able to pour in spiritual

---

7. David Morehouse, *Psychic Warrior* (New York: St. Martin's, 1998).

power, others, using similar methods, are trying to undermine our morale.[8]

Armed and red-robed, to express the power of Mars, the angelic presences they invoked were set patrolling Britain from north to south, east to west, protecting the nation's shoreline at a time when invasion seemed imminent. After a couple of months of intense inner effort, the line of defence was pushed out to the minefields which lay along the Norwegian coast, down the length of the North Sea, pushing out all that was malign and keeping the darkness at bay.

Who better to summon in those times and that place but sword-wielding King Arthur, the Once and Future King, summoning him from his long sleep in the cave under Glastonbury Tor, and bringing with him Merlin, the arch-mage of Britain with his diamond sceptre. If anyone could sort out the Nazis, they could.

She spent a lot of time, too, rising in vision from the mystic Cave within the heart of the British psyche, and climbing up through it by a winding staircase, past the Hall of Learning which was seen as a great mediaeval library, past the Chapel of the Grail above that, and higher yet to the Watchtower.

This Watchtower stood upon the mountain top. Here, if one had great nerve, one was permitted to join the mysterious cloaked and hooded Watcher who was always there. Here, if one could bear the pressure, one was allowed to stare into the change-winds of good and evil, into the heart of the storm that was sweeping across the world, and get prophetic glimpses of things yet to come. This was no place for the beginner, she warned.

These were more than mere pictures in the head. These were real beings, real places, operating and existing on real levels, and in 1940 she was describing how during bombing and anti-aircraft fire she

---

8. Dion Fortune (edited by Gareth Knight), *The Magical Battle of Britain* (Bradford on Avon, UK: Golden Gates Press), p 37.

was able to see the Invisible Helpers at work that they had invoked, adding:

> There were also presences of a higher and more intellectual grade who seemed to be holding lines of power taut under great tension. Over all was the iridescent dome of protection guarded by great angelic presences. These are among the things we have been visualising and building on the astral, and at the moment of testing it was a wonderful experience to see how potent and tangible they were . . . .[9]

As the Blitz in the outer world intensified, she advised:

> When the actual bombing starts, or the sound of gunfire is alarmingly near, go into meditation, if possible assuming the meditation posture. If preparations have been made in advance, it will prove unexpectedly easy, for the stress of an air raid heightens psychic perception, and many a person will witness the parting of the Veil and see into the Unseen who, under normal conditions, might have to work long before they achieved such an experience . . . [10]

You have to admire her. She had *hwyl*, as her Welsh husband would have said, which is an untranslatable Welsh word invoking spirit, fire, courage, and zest.

It was not all the inner planes. In her letter to 'HF', she confided:

> There is also at the present time a definite attack gong on, not just on us. I will tell you a queer story some day. It concerns the mystic side of Nazism. It is not fantasy. I can show you papers with the name of a Munich printer carefully obliterated, brought into the country for the purpose of subverting the group mind of the race, and tell you of a man who is second generation of those who,

---

9. Fortune, *Magical Battle of Britain*, p. 41.
10. Gareth Knight, *Dion Fortune and the Inner Light* (Loughborough, UK: Thoth Publications, 2000).

though domiciled in Germany, and in everything German, even to blood, retained British citizenship in order to be able to come in and do this work.[11]

It seems that Dion, through her many contacts with the intelligence network in Britain (including possibly Crowley himself), had become aware of a Nazi 'sleeper' agent whose activities were now being carefully monitored. She concludes by adding almost apologetically to her friend: 'So you see what you let yourself in for through being legal advisor to a witch!'

As late as 27 March 1945, however, she was asking Crowley's advice about some matter which seems to have involved a psychic attack which had obviously disturbed even her very greatly. His reply began:

> Dear D.F.
> 93
> I am very concerned indeed at what you tell me. It is your second near escape and I really think it might be a warning. I have never been a partisan of the Hero Martyr School. The Captain should not be the last person to be saved or go down with the ship. He is the person to be saved first because he is the best witness as to the causes of the accident and that may be valuable to the cause of navigation in general . . .

It is hard to tell from the rest of his lengthy and concerned reply exactly what the situation had been, but the essence of his response was: *Don't worry. This really happened. Have been there, too. Get over it.* He ended: 'I do hope you will take my advice and get well outside of range until we have driven the Hun out of the Hague and neighbourhood despite all that the bishop can do'.

---

11. Personal collection of Maria Babwahsingh.

And what about Crowley himself? How did he conduct his war? On the surface his approach was tamer. But then again he was in his late sixties, had been wrestling with his heroin addiction for the previous twenty-five years, and didn't have quite as much fire left within. It is said that all magicians become mystics in the end. This is not so much that they become disenchanted with their rituals, but more a case that they don't have the same huge levels of energy required for walking the circle, and directing power, and travelling the planes. However, on a differing level he was every bit as busy as DF.

As already noted, Crowley had been an effective double agent working for the Secret Intelligence Service for many years. Although the unheralded highlight of his work had been done with great effect during the war of 1914–18, various covert government departments still continued to use him to gain insights into those many continental occult groups involved in subversive and revolutionary politics. The Germans by the time of the Second World War had become aware of Crowley's true loyalties, and referred to him in their files with complete distrust as the 'high-grade Freemason Aleister Crowley'. Even so he still had many followers in the occult circles there until the total crackdown by Himmler, which is why he would have still been useful to the British authorities even if they felt that—drug-riddled as he was—he may not have seemed quite as reliable these days as they might have wished. Plus, he does seem to have made extraordinarily brave but covert visits into the Reich itself during the late 1930s.

He was certainly close to senior figures within British Military Intelligence, and seems to have been used in what became known as 'Operation Mistletoe', devised by Ian Fleming (author of the James Bond novels). There are those who feel this never happened. Others insist that it most certainly did. The story is as follows:

Together, Fleming and Crowley organised Sappers—military engineers—to clear a circle and an avenue of trees in the Ashdown Forest. Then, orchestrating Canadian soldiers dressed in improvised robes which bore mystical sigils, overshadowed by a massive image of Hitler, they performed what seemed to be an awesome rite. The crucial thing was that two undercover German agents codenamed 'Kestrel' and 'Sea Eagle', contacted via the Romanian Mission in London, had been invited to attend the impressive ceremonies. When they passed on their observations to the Deputy Führer Rudolf Hess, who was as deeply involved in things occult as Himmler, they helped persuade him that the Order of the Golden Dawn was not only alive and well, but part of a genuine Peace Party in Britain, whose head was the Duke of Hamilton. Hess was convinced that Britain could be persuaded to join Germany in Hitler's apocalyptic struggle against Soviet Russia.

Fleming and other members of the SIS then created a disinformation campaign of various astrologers predicting a 'momentous event' that would occur on 10 May 1941, making sure that all these announcements reached the ears of the Deputy Führer, who planned his historic flight to Britain accordingly, quite certain that on arrival he would have a private meeting with King George VI and other luminaries, and that peace would be made with the British. He was certain about this because he had had a dream of exactly this happening, and took it as a vision of the future. This has led some to speculate that Crowley had used his magick to get inside Hess's mind. Again, this was something that the CIA later experimented with—and successfully—at great length, so we should not dismiss it as absurd.

In the event, Hess landed in Scotland and was arrested and driven to the MI5 headquarters in London to be interrogated. Fleming's suggestion to Churchill that Aleister Crowley was the man best qualified to deal with Hess was brushed aside. At least officially. Unofficially it seems he might have spent three weeks interrogating him at a top-secret establishment known as Latchmere House, with unknown results. It is quite likely that he used mescaline, as a kind of truth drug.

On the other side of the English Channel, meanwhile, the Nazi Party promptly disowned Hess when they realised what had gone on and gone wrong, and wrote their high and solo flyer off as a mad occultist acting on his own. The man himself spent the rest of his long life in various jails.

However much truth there was to the whole story, the verifiable fact is that the both Crowley and Fortune had contacts at very high levels within that shadow world of espionage and counter-espionage as a whole. As Richard Spence has shown in his book *Secret Agent 666*, a large number of the names in Crowley's Magical Diaries actually refer to meetings with people who were active members of intelligence services across Europe and America. They were not visiting to talk about Magick, or to reminisce about the good old days.

In fact, several members of Dion Fortune's Fraternity of the Inner Light and Aleister Crowley's O. T. O. and A. A. were also members of various branches of British Military Intelligence. If they were not using actual magickal powers on astral levels, then they were applying their insight into human psychology to create effective 'black' propaganda that would infect the enemy's will to fight.

Understand that neither DF nor AC were what might be termed 'fluffy' magicians, sending out waves of goodwill and forgiveness toward the double-headed monstrous eagle of the Third Reich. Instead, they sought to destroy this creature before it got to them. They sought to shatter the sinister *hakenkreuz*, or swastika, with their own beautiful—and powerful—rose-cross.

Whatever the truth about the story of Crowley and the Hess plot, the sheer myth of it has a life and value of its own on magical levels.

⁓

What is certain and material, however, is that despite his financial straits, his deepening heroin addiction and related health problems, not to mention the stress caused by the constant danger of bombing, Aleister Crowley brought out at this time his wonderful *Book of Thoth* in collaboration with the artist Freida Harris.

Lady Freida Harris was never one of his Scarlet Women, nor even one of his occasional sexual partners (*lover* is often too wrong a word for many of these people in Crowley's life). But she drew upon the very best of the Master Therion's vision and created a tarot pack which makes all others before and since look wimpish.

One of those to whom he tried to sell the book, but who said she couldn't afford the huge price of ten guineas, was Maiya Tranchell Hayes, who was an extremely important figure in the life of Dion Fortune, and a crucial link between her and Crowley. On the caduceus, she can be found at one of those junctures on the shaft of light where the twin serpents of DF and AC cross. If there are any secrets or mysteries or conundrums involved in the relationship between Aleister Crowley and Dion Fortune, then they would be explained by this woman, whose Magical Name was Ex Fide Fortis.[12]

Maiya was at this time the wife of Dr Edmund Duncan Tranchell Hayes, who worked at Northampton County Mental Hospital. She had been Dion's initiator and mentor in the Alpha et Omega Temple of the Golden Dawn and was said to be the inspiration for the exotic, ageless, artistic, and bohemian character of Vivien le Fay Morgan, as described in The Sea Priestess and Moon Magic. As the male narrator in the former notes: 'The sea-priestess, it seemed, was a kind of pythoness, and the gods spoke through her. Being a pythoness, she was negative, passive; she did not make magic herself, but was an instrument in the hands of priests, and however perfect an instrument she might be, there was no use in her if there was not one to use her'.[13] It was not the austere Egyptian faith which she worked with, 'nor the radiant gods of Greece, but the primordial Brythonic cult that had its roots in Atlantis, which the dark Ionian Kelt shares with Breton and Basque'.[14]

---

12. As she left an estate worth nearly £11,000, it might be thought be that she was avoiding being stung by the Beast for financial support.

13. Dion Fortune, The Sea Priestess (London: SIL, 1990), p. 117. First published in 1938.

14. Ibid., p. 136.

Maiya was in fact Irish, the daughter of a solicitor.

In the 1920s they had done early experiments in trance medium-ship. When she re-appeared in the younger woman's life in the 1940s to do an even deeper level of work, they developed it into what was later called the Arthurian Formula, part of which involved 'polarity workings' between an older woman and a younger man. Quite apart from the alignment with the archetypal figures from the Arthurian cultus, this may have been based upon direct personal experience, because Dr Edmund Duncan Tranchell Hayes (her second husband) was some years younger than Maiya.

The work she began doing with Dion now, during the war, seemed to involve toying with the structure of a new Order which their inner guide told them would supersede the Fraternity of the Inner Light, although this does not seem to have happened—on the outer planes at least. In this new set-up there was a three-fold function of Maiya being designated Star, Dion taking on the Moon energies, and William K. Creasy being the Earth aspect. The Sun was represented by an inner being known as Shemesh—which was more a title meaning the Sun than a personal name, and which was involved in 'remaking the Order for the Aquarian Age. There is always a Shemesh, the Teacher, and Hakim, the Healer—he is still to come. We build the Temple of the New Age'.[15]

In fact, a being known as Ara ben Shemesh first appeared within the magic of the Golden Dawn as early as 1908, when Dr Robert Felkin and his wife Ethel managed to make contact with him. Ithell Colquhoun described the entity as a '... discarnate Arab who claimed affiliation with the desert-temple visited by Father Christian Rosenkreutz on his Middle Eastern pilgrimage. Felkin, realising a magical sodality's need for contact with the inner planes, accepted Ara ben

---

15. Gareth Knight, *Dion Fortune and the Inner Light*, p. 256.

Shemesh as his teacher and the latter's "Sun-Masters" as his Secret Chiefs'.[16]

There can be no doubt that this is the same being.

Looking through the communications at that time, Gareth Knight, who has probably forgotten more about magic than most of us will ever know, commented with astonishment: 'The implications of this are quite staggering. The communicator seems fully to be expecting a complete take over of the Fraternity of the Inner Light, with Dion Fortune regarded as very much a second fiddle . . . '[17] He goes on to add:

> This series of meetings went on under conditions of intense secrecy, although somewhat infrequently in the beginning. Another meeting was held in December [1940] in which general plans were revealed as to what was to be known as 'the Nameless order'—the title chosen for the sake of dignity and because names had been so much abused in the past.[18]

What was this inner 'Nameless Order'? Surely it was Crowley's A. A. —the Order of the Silver Star? Was Maiya seen, for a brief time at least, as something akin to the secret Imperator of the FIL? Did they want to keep it 'Nameless' so as not to terrify the less enlightened members of the Inner Light—especially the teeny-weenies in their outer court? This would explain Crowley's letter to Frederic Mellinger after Dion's death: 'With her I had an arrangement by which she acknowledged my authority, but she was wisely or rather prudently, most anxious to keep this fact secret from her own followers on account of the old nonsense . . . A great deal of difficult negotiation is necessary in order to pick up her following'.[19]

---

16. Ithell Colquhoun, *The Sword of Wisdom* (London: Neville Spearman, 1975).

17. Gareth Knight, *Dion Fortune and the Inner Light*, p. 255.

18. Ibid., p. 255.

19. O. T. O. archives.

In the event, Maiya seems to have faded out of the picture at this point, although there are memories of her as a guest-elder in the FIL in the 1940s, attending some of the ceremonies behind a veil or a screen. Perhaps as the work progressed she found out that her former pupil had now surpassed her in magical skill and status, and so stepped aside. Or perhaps the death of her young husband c. 1941 was a body blow. As it was, although her extraordinary character provided the inspiration for the heroine of Dion Fortune's best novels, in the eyes of most people today the qualities of the Atlantean Sea Priestess have become those of Dion Fortune's own spirit.

The workings they did, before this blending of their psyches and personas, are detailed in Gareth Knight's *The Secret Tradition in Arthurian Legend*, and the annoyingly coy use of the term 'polarity workings' was perhaps a means of distancing themselves from the Crowleyan label of Sex Magick—for that is what they were, even though it was deemed to be on a higher level than mere rutting. Maiya, using the Magical Name Ishtar, was the force behind these. Hope Hughes, of the Hermes Temple, had once taken fright and suspected that DF had turned 'Black' because she had heard reports of a naked woman being used in rites within DF's home at 3 Queensborough Terrace, London (known invariably as 3QT). If that story is true, it would be surprising if the lady involved was *not* Maiya.

On the other hand, Christine Hartley, who at that time was not on the same level as her teacher, told me that she and Kim Seymour had been involved in high-grade rites within 3QT which involved a certain degree of 'intimate contact' as she said—which might have made the teeny-weenies go rushing to the doors had they glimpsed it. The fact is, all such polarity workings involve 'magick', whether people are comfortable with the Crowleyan overtones of this word or not.

The relevance to the present book is that, like Dion Fortune, Maiya Tranchell Hayes' name had also appeared on the list of those deemed worthy of receiving the equinoctial Word. She also began her two surviving but inconsequential letters to Crowley with the telling 'Do What Thou Wilt shall be the whole of the Law' and ended them as required with 'Love is the Law; Love under Will', while addressing him as G. H., which means 'Greatly Honoured' (or 'God Head', depending on whose ego is involved). Make no mistake, she did not do this out of politeness. She did it because she was acknowledging his authority. She was writing to him as a Thelemite. Is this an indication that both Maiya and Dion were closer to what might be called the Thelemic Current than previously imagined? All Crowleyans would give a might cry of *Yes!* Many admirers of Dion Fortune will quiver and quibble at the very thought.

However, whatever they thought of Crowley the Magus, that self-styled 'chosen Priest and Apostle of Infinite Space', they would not have liked the poem that Crowley the Man wrote in Maiya's honour, included in his unpublished *Book Of Oaths*. She was known to him then by the formal name of her first marriage to Dr John Curtis Webb.

The Fly Catcher
(*Mrs Curtis Webb*)

Aristocrat or pimply Pleb
Are all the same to Mrs Webb;
She pays me, I've never paid her,
I 'played' the bitch, and then I 'made' her;
Harridan or blushing deb
Are all the same to Mrs Webb

In the ritualistic farces
She's the one to smack the arses;
They crawl a mile, then sprawl a while
To fit them for the rank and vile;

How Heavenly Mansions can they win
If they despise the House of Sin?

As with the great, so with the least
All must pay tribute to the Beast.

[*And so on . . . The final verse is rather better known:*]

Mrs Webb does what she can
As a lusty Lesbian
To make Sappho of the filly
Who never trots in Piccadilly;
Girl to girl and man to man,
Is part and pattern of her plan;
Lad to lass and lass to lad
(bread to bread alone, is bad);
So the changes she must ring,
If the angels are to sing.
Aristo' and putrid pleb.,
Harridan and dainty Deb.,
There's never one that misses web(b).[20]

At first reading this is a rather distasteful and not at all clever piece of verse which seems to be downright insulting to Mrs W. However, it is not much different to the verses he wrote about himself, detailing his own self-abasement as a means of dealing with things that horrified him, and especially in respect to his own homosexual magick with Victor Neuburg, in which he often took the feminine role as 'Alys'. In context, this may well be Crowley's odd way of showing respect, and mentioning things that were—then—unmentionable. And it may well be, also,

---

20. This poem appears on www.lashtal.com (accessed 3 August 2009), and is from the still unpublished *Book of Oaths*. It is used here with the kind permission of William Breeze.

that Crowley was just making unjustified accusations against someone who did not deserve it. Something that he did often.

The importance of the verse, however, is that it clarifies (albeit indirectly) Dion Fortune's own sexual orientations. Even today, because the rumours of Dion's sexual ambivalence still hang around like an earthbound spirit, this is a point worth making, because after all if a pope had turned out to be a woman in disguise, the world might want to know, if only out of sheer delighted curiosity.[21]

In her own day she was seen as having a distinct mannishness. In fact a correspondent of mine described how his father had known young DF and insisted that 'she' was a man in drag. However she confronted this head-on her classic book *Psychic Self-Defence*, which was more an autobiography than a book on dealing with astral attacks. She noted with apparent amusement that she had once been accused of being a man in disguise, and that the charge had found believers! Crowley never made much secret about his own active bisexuality, and was quite happy to take any such insults on the chin; but it must have been difficult for a young and often uncertain woman like Violet, trying to find a style for herself, to hear that kind of charge.

As she became more involved in magical work, however, she became aware that we are all two-sexed beings. She knew that it was part of the Mysteries to look for the woman within the man and the man within the woman. Today, because of the pioneering writings of people like Jung, Freud, D. H. Lawrence, and Crowley himself, that is almost taken for granted, yet it was heady stuff in those early days. As she wrote in *The Sea Priestess*: 'But the ancients did not concern themselves with anomalies, but said that the soul was bisexual, and that as one or the other aspect manifested in the world of form, the alternative aspect was latent in the world of the spirit'.

She was aware, too, of the attraction she had for women of a certain persuasion, and patiently explained that where the leader of a

---

21. There is the legendary figure of 'Pope Joan', who supposedly reigned in the 850s.

magical group is a woman, then that person will get a lot of unstable people of her own sex abreacting their passions for her.

Christine Hartley, who knew her very well, was at no point subjected to any kind of lesbian approach. Not that it would have worried her much if it had happened. Despite the rumours that I heard, second-hand, that Dion Fortune indulged in sexual relationships with both sexes in her final years, and had a full-blown lesbian fling with Maiya, there is no evidence for any of it, and no one these days would turn a hair in any case—thanks in no small part to the pioneering libido of the Great Beast.

So the plain and crude fact is: if Dion Fortune had been a man in drag, then Crowley would have sniffed it out at once. If she had been a closet lesbian, he would have made some sharp observation about this in print somewhere.

~

On the level of normal human loving and all its concerns, Mr and Mrs Evans ceased to be a couple, and Penry left Violet some years before the end of this period. He and his new wife, Dr Anne Mower White, then lived quite happily ever after in a house named 'Pan', in Amersham, Buckinghamshire, and he did good work—great work—with disadvantaged children in particular. People have tended to trivialise him over the years, writing him off as little more than 'Dion Fortune's husband', effectively brushing his shade aside in the urge to marvel at his wife. Yet the fact is, as a human being, Thomas Penry Evans exemplified the motto of the Fraternity of the Inner Light: 'I desire to Know, in order to Serve'. Really, he was one of the Shining Ones.

And whatever torments their marriage bed might have held for them both, at least the first Mrs Evans seems to have found enough fulfilment on various sorts of levels in her final years, war or no war.

Which is something that the Master Therion was never quite able to achieve, never really managing to escape from that aspect of his magickal persona known as Alastor—Wanderer of the Wastes, for the women (and men) came and went in his odd life, and never seemed to leave much warmth.

So the full truth of the relationship between Aleister Crowley and Dion Fortune during the war years may never be known, but the fact is they waged battles in their own souls while defeating the Nazis on the inner levels, and the results are with us today.

chapter three

PRIESTS AND PRIESTESSES

In some ways the decade before they met, from the late 1920s to the 1930s, was the highest and most successful period for that construct known as Dion Fortune, and a very troublesome one for Aleister Crowley.

She had fallen out with the Theosophical Society which until then had been almost all-pervasive in its influence on many aspects of British occultism. The point of contention was that the TS leader, Annie Besant, had been devoting the society's entire energies into championing a messiah in the form of young Jiddhu Krishnamurti. Plus, Dion by this time had also broken free of the Hermetic Order of the Golden Dawn, in which she had originally been initiated, and was now fully in charge of her own Fraternity of the Inner Light. In magical terms this would have meant that she was now at least an Adeptus Minor, and had made inner contacts with what she would have termed her own 'Masters'. In fact, the whole lodge revolved around and in many ways depended upon her own exceptional mediumship.

One of the things not appreciated today is the fact that the archaic Witchcraft Act of 1735 was still in place in Britain, and not repealed until 1951. It was still possible to be prosecuted for pretending to 'exercise or use any kind of witchcraft, sorcery, enchantment, or conjuration, or undertake to tell fortunes'. Supposed contact with spirits fell into this category. As late as 1944 Helen Duncan was branded a witch and spy 'guilty of revealing wartime secrets' by an Old Bailey jury because of potentially sensitive information that she disclosed—'allegedly via contacts with the spirit world'. For those whose lives revolved around exactly this, a certain degree of caution was required in the way the Mysteries were made public.

Despite this, the year 1927 was an important one for Dion Fortune: against all the odds she found herself a good man and was married to Penry Evans in April of that year. This period marked the start of her major books, not to mention the monthly articles she wrote for the *Inner Light* magazine, and it began with publication of *The Problem of Purity*, which was her last book under her maiden name, and which reflects some of the counselling advice she once offered people in the early days of psychology, in a sexually guilt-ridden society. Again, it was a striking and risqué offering from a young woman at that time, but seems frequently risible and extremely tame by the standards of today.

This year also saw the publication of her first novel *The Demon Lover*, which was a cracking yarn about an innocent heroine, Veronica Mainwaring, a natural psychic who is entrapped by a morally corrupt adept to spy upon his masters on the astral plane. This led to all kinds of bizarre happenings of etheric vampirism that are counteracted by even more drastic means. Her intention, she later said, was to write a thriller pure and simple, but in the course of writing it ended up as a kind of saga of the purification of the soul through initiation. As her main interpreter Gareth Knight commented: '. . . it stands apart from her later novels insofar that she is here looking at occultism in the light of psychology—whereas in the later novels she has moved on to interpret psychology in the light of occultism. This was her own assertion, and there is indeed quite a profound difference between her earlier and later fictional work'.[1] Not least being the fact that she had learned her craft over the years.

She was living with her doctor husband in 3QT, which provided both living quarters and a functioning temple devoted to the Western Mysteries, and was about to buy another place called Chalice Orchard, at the foot of Glastonbury Tor. This mystic hill had enormous importance for her. According to legend the top of it was a gathering point for the Wild Hunt; inside it was a cave in which the mighty King Arthur lay sleeping, waiting for the call to arms when his nation needed him. It still draws people today, due in no small part to the magical work she did there.

By 1930 the FIL had established three degrees of the Lesser Mysteries, and Dion Fortune was able to withdraw to work more on the inner levels, for her own needs—the role of Magus of the Lodge being taken over by Penry Evans.

Then from 1931–35 she began work on a manuscript that was to become The Mystical Qabalah—still one of the best books on the topic, three generations later.

Apart from these her literary output in that decade was impressive, though it was dwarfed in comparison with Crowley's. On the other hand, he had time on his hands to devote entirely to writing. Alan Burnett-Rae, who spent some years in the role of long-suffering landlord to Crowley, recalled how, in the mid-1930s, letters would pour into the flat in Welbeck Street addressed to 'Sir Aleister Crowley', or other of his previous identities such Lord Boleskine, the Comte de St Germain, quite apart from the Great Beast 666, Priest of the Princes, etc. 'He always asserted that he was of "Earth's First Blood", an aristocrat and a genius. He complained or boasted when reduced to poverty, or relative poverty, that he had never been brought up to work and was therefore now unable to'. This was one of the disadvantages

---

1. 'Gareth Knight. About Dion Fortune', online at http://www.angelfire.com/az/garethknight/dfbooks.html (accessed 4 August 2009).

that Crowley had been cursed with: he had never had a job; he never had to learn the normal give and take of human relationships within the workplace, or develop what Dion Fortune described as the social and marital lubricant of pure courtesy.

Despite first appearances neither Fortune nor Crowley were what might be called 'professional occultists', which are, alas, far more prevalent at the beginning of the twenty-first century than they were in their day. (In fact, the British have long had an inherent distrust of such beings.) That is to say they did not charge large sums for teaching, or bring money in by giving grand initiations that were priced proportionate to the candidate's likely bank balance. Although the Beast had to earn to live, no one ever doubted that Magick came before Money, and that the Gods of the Prophet came before the God of Profit. There were many occasions when he was genuinely outraged that his initiates had abused their status and sought dominion over others for personal gain. DF was especially scathing of 'certain American organisations' which she saw as being little more than money-making rackets, and she refused to call them Orders. Her prime target here was AMORC, the Ancient and Mystical Order Rosae Crucis, founded by H. Spencer Lewis in 1915. Crowley also had a shot at this same target in his *Confessions*, where he writes about 'one of the charlatans who worked the Rosicrucian racket', and without naming Lewis directly goes on to describe and dismiss his claims, but adding that he was a good chap at heart and by no means altogether ignorant of Magick.

Neither of them made much from their writing either. Although she was able to find publishers easily enough, her books sold modestly, in the low hundreds. In contrast, because of his foul reputation, AC invariably had to self-publish, often charging below cost, and saw his works sell dismally if at all. The former managed with the money from her marriage settlement and an inheritance from her grandfather; the latter with an income from, as we will shall see, a man called Karl Germer, plus erratic and indeterminate sums from

British Intelligence. If you loaned Crowley money, you would never see it returned.

⁓

While DF was maintaining a low profile in the world, except for occasional public lectures on a wide variety of esoteric topics, the whole world was aware of the Great Beast.

In 1928 while living in Paris he had written both his classic *Magick in Theory and Practice* and his strange novel *Moonchild*, and managed to find himself a publisher for these in P. R. Stephenson, who had previously championed the shocking offerings from D. H. Lawrence. To his delight these were both published a year later. What he never realised was that a certain Mrs Evans had been working hard behind the scenes to try and get *Magick* accepted by the respectable Rider and Co. After a meeting on 19 June with the senior editor, Mr Strutton, and using all her powers of persuasion to get him to accept it, she then offered to go through the manuscript (which Gerald Yorke had sent her), cutting out what she called the 'unacceptables' and then re-typing it so that it would be ready for immediate publication. In the event, it was still too much for Rider, and Stephenson's tiny Mandrake Press took it on, partly financed by an exasperated Yorke.

The book had a print run of 3000 copies but only attracted seven subscribers. Dion publicly reviewed it and described it as having a very uneven literary quality, containing 'much grossness and ribaldry, like all Crowley's writings, and much of it deliberately obscure and allusive'.[2] No doubt these are the parts she would have cut out, without—as she felt it—damaging the essential text. Lawrence Sutin, Crowley's best biographer, disagrees with this assessment. To him *Magick* was a modernist masterwork, and Dion Fortune made her comments because she was mirroring the prudishness of the time.

---

2. Quoted in Lawrence Sutin, *Do What Thou Wilt: A Life of Aleister Crowley* (New York: St. Martin's, 2000), p. 348.

And Lon Milo DuQuette also made an important observation when he wrote: 'Like all of us, Crowley had many flaws and shortcomings. The greatest of those, in my opinion, was his inability to understand that everyone else in the world was not as educated and clever as he. It is clear, even in his earliest works, he often took fiendish delight in terrifying those who were either too lazy, too bigoted, or too slow-witted to understand him'.[3]

However, on top of all this, what many of the transatlantic readers never realised is how often Crowley would insert what W. E. Butler termed *pince-sans-rire* jokes (deadpan, in other words) of the purely English kind, which were taken at face value.

While Dion in that later letter apologised to Crowley for not being as smart as he assumed, in this instance she was less concerned with the style and morals within *Magick* than with what she, as an Adeptus, saw between the lines. She went on to write in a technical vein:

> The formulae, too, on which he works, would be considered averse and evil by occultists accustomed to the Qabalistic tradition, for he uses 11 instead of 10 as the basis of his batteries of knocks in the magical ceremonies, and 11 is the number of the Qlipoth, or Evil Sephiroth; a battery of 11, therefore, is an invocation of the Qlipoth. No hint of this is given in the text, and it is an ugly trap for the unwary student.
>
> Crowley has, however, a remarkable insight into the philosophy of occultism, and when he expounds this, he is a most illuminating writer, and I, for one, would not wish to minimise my debt to his writings; his practical methods, however, are another matter, and are, in my opinion, too dangerous to meddle with in any shape or form.[4]

---

3. Lon Milo DuQuette, *The Magick of Aleister Crowley* (York Beach, ME: Weiser, 2003), p. 5–6.

4. Dion Fortune, 'The Occult Field Today', in *Applied Magic* (York Beach, ME: Weiser, 2000), p. 65.

⌣

In this year also, 1930, Crowley married the exotic and sorely troubled Maria Teresa de Miramar, who became his second wife. With initial enthusiasm he called her his High Priestess of Voodoo, but it went wrong very quickly. Within a year he had found a new lover, Hanni Jaeger, a nineteen-year-old German artist. Crowley wrote to his wife, 'You should get a divorce—find a man who will stand for your secret drinking and your scandalous behaviour'. Like his first wife, Rose, Maria Teresa was admitted to a mental hospital suffering from the delusion that she was the daughter of the king and queen. Whether she had been a disturbed soul before she met Crowley, or after, is a moot point. When she told her doctors she was also Mrs Aleister Crowley, this was taken as a further symptom of her madness.

Before this, however, possibly because the sister of one of his disciples had written to the French authorities complaining about the despicable Englishman in their midst, he and his new partner found themselves being expelled from France. Even today it is not clear why. French occultism has always been inseparable from French politics, and the real or reputed proclivities of the *Raspoutine anglais* or the *Mage noir* would hardly have shocked them too much. On the other hand, one small journal did say that he had been booted out because he had been acting as a secret agent for Germany. In fact, as Richard Spence points out: 'A connection between Crowley and German intelligence may not have been a fantasy spun by the Gallic press . . . his key devotee in Germany, Karl Germer, had at least a past association with Berlin's secret services'.[5] Yet his protestations of having been a double agent must have run true somewhere, because his assigned case officer from British Intelligence, Gerald Yorke, and a senior official in the same called Arthur Burbury, ensured that he was eventually allowed back into Britain without any fuss. As Yorke

---

5. Richard B. Spence, *Secret Agent 666*, p. 205.

pointed out to a senior figure in Scotland Yard: 'the Beast was not as beastly as he made out to be'.

This was something that Dion Fortune, in her cloistered life, also took into account. As she wrote in the *Inner Light* magazine:

> But while I entirely dissociate myself from Crowley's methods, I would not wish to minimise his contribution to occult literature, which is of the highest value. From his books the advanced student, who knows how to read between the lines and refine the gold from the dross, can learn an immense amount, and if our interest is limited to an author's writings, we need not concern ourselves with his personal character or private life . . . [6]

His private life was never particularly private at all. This was partly because of his newsworthiness, and also because of his classic *The Confessions of Aleister Crowley: An Autohagiography*, which came out in 1930 and was divided into six sections, entitled:

1. Towards the Golden Dawn
2. The Mystical Adventure
3. The Advent of the Aeon of Horus
4. Magical Workings
5. The Magus
6. At the Abbey of Thelema

The original printing in 1929 by Mandrake Press only included the first two volumes, but all printings since 1969 have included all six. It gives an intimate portrait of Crowley and also of an age. As a book it is clever, verging on the brilliant, pompous blending into the sardonic, delightfully and startlingly esoteric, and filled with unfailingly superb self-confidence. It appeals to mountaineers, magicians,

6. Dion Fortune, 'The Occult Field Today', reprinted in *Applied Magic*, p. 66.

hedonists, scoundrels, adventurers, libertines, and drug addicts. Or as John Symonds recorded him as saying: 'I am the Beast, I am the Word of the Aeon. I spend my soul in blazing torrents that roar into Night, streams that with molten tongues hiss as they lick. I am a hell of a Holy Guru'.[7]

While that last strikes a wondrous note, like the sort that might have come from his Magick Bell, it describes Crowley the Mage. It is always worth bearing in mind his own assessment of Crowley the Man when he wrote: 'Have I ever done anything of value or am I a mere trifler, existing by a series of shifts of one kind or another? A wastrel, coward, man of straw? I can find no answer whatever, the obvious verdict being "Guilty"'.[8]

At the same time, in 1930, Dion Fortune was writing her own auto-biography, although it was never marketed as that. The book in question was given the (for that era) hugely weird title of *Psychic Self-Defence*, and subtitled *A Study in Occult Pathology and Criminality*. Many of her books were simply collections of essays on a rough theme, but this one was purpose-built. It was less a treatise on defence against malign entities than a magical autobiography. It is a unique book, bizarre in places, and one which gives enough detail to make the events believable, but never quite enough for the characters to be recognised. After all, many of them were still very much alive, and there was always the danger of libel. In sections, it is also a very beautiful book, showing the first glimpse of the peculiar rhythms she later used with such great effect in her final two novels:

> I have had my full share of the adventures of the Path; have known men and women who could indubitably be ranked as adepts; seen phenomena such as no seance room has ever known, and borne

---

7. John Symonds, *The Great Beast* (London: Mayflower, 1973).
8. Ibid.

my share in it; taken part in psychic feuds, and stood my watch on the roster of the occult police force which, under the Masters of the Great White Lodge, keeps guard over the nations, each according to its race; kept the occult vigil when one dare not sleep while the sun is below the horizon; and hung on desperately, matching my staying-power against the attack until the moon-tides changed and the force of the onslaught blew itself out.

And through all these experiences I was learning to interpret occultism in the light of psychology and psychology in the light of occultism, the one counterchecking and explaining the other.[9]

So she never lost touch with her own human insights, despite the extraordinary adventures on inner levels.

By this time, in the mid-1930s, her three temples were fully functioning on outer and inner levels: she had the headquarters of the Fraternity at 3QT, plus the pilgrim centre known as the 'Chalice Orchard Club' in Glastonbury, along with that temple known as The Belfry, dedicated to the Mysteries of Isis, in West London.

Crowley in contrast had a series of rooms in various flats across London from which he was constantly being ejected for failure to pay his bills. Then again, as any true Mage knows, the real temples are internal and exist in realms other than the physical and can be accessed likewise. Lack of such a base did not cause him to pause in his practice of Magick during this period, and he certainly never lacked people willing to work with or for him. One of these was Israel Regardie . . .

Israel Regardie was born in 1907 to a family of Orthodox Jewish immigrants in the slums of London's East End. In 1921 they emigrated again, to America this time, where he harboured dreams of becoming an artist, although it was his discovery of the works of H. P. Blavatsky

---

9. Dion Fortune, *Psychic Self-Defence* (York Beach, ME: Weiser, 2001), p. xxv. First published in 1930.

and all things esoteric which really fired his spirit. In March 1926 he was initiated into the Neophyte grade of the Washington College of the 'Societas Rosicruciana in America', or SRIA. By June he had advanced to the Zelator grade. It was all going so well—and then he read Crowley's *Book Four* and it became *very* strange indeed.

After receiving the young man's letter, Crowley invited him to join him in Paris where he became Crowley's secretary and general dogsbody. The Beast's method of initiating the prudish young virgin into the ways of Thelemic learning took an unexpected step on the very first night when, after coffee and cognac, Crowley and his lover Kasimira Bass fell to the floor and had sex '. . . like a pair of animals right there in front of me'.[10] As Lawrence Sutin noted, as a means of dealing with something like puritanism, this direct confrontation with psychic *bête noires* was a hallmark of Crowley's teaching.

In the event, although Regardie tried to get his employer to teach him the magical arts, he failed to get very far. So he continued to study magic on his own, reading every grimoire, article, or manuscript that was available to him. When the Beast was ejected from France, Regardie's employment came to an end.

Despite a rancorous parting, Regardie tried to repair Crowley's by-now-completely-grubby public image by co-authoring a book with P. R. Stephenson called *The Legend of Aleister Crowley*, which sought to redress the balance and show that the Master Therion was more sinned against than sinning. To a certain extent this was true: Crowley then was like the celebrities who suffer the bear-baiting of the tabloid press today, whose every move, every utterance, is subject to scrutiny and spin of the most vicious kind.

Regardie, who never became a true Thelemite but remained what he called 'a Golden Dawn man' to the end of his life, then began writing his own books, and was able to survive because of the contracts

---

10. Israel Regardie, *The Eye in the Triangle: An Interpretation of Aleister Crowley* (Phoenix, AZ: Falcon Press, 1982).

given for *The Tree of Life* and *Garden of Pomegranates*. This was when he came into contact with Dion Fortune.

In a letter dated 1 November 1932, she writes to Regardie from 3QT:

> Riders have just sent me both your books with the request that I will do an article on them, and this I am now at work on. I think very highly of both the books, and especially 'The Tree of Life'. It is quite the best book on magic, in my opinion, not excepting either Crowley or Levi. I think it is an exceedingly fine piece of work.
>
> I am sorry there is no chance of meeting you in the near future: I think a talk would have been very interesting. Ceremonial magic is a matter that especially interests me, and we are well equipped both here and at our Glastonbury centre for doing it. Glastonbury is particularly interesting for workings, as our place is on the side of the Tor, the 'Hill of Vision'. Perhaps some time you will be able to visit us there.
>
> I judge from the correspondences given in 'The Garden of Pomegranates' that you are using the old 'Golden Dawn System', which is the one I use myself. I think it is far and away the best. Crowley gives it away in 777, but I also have the Mathers MSS to check it by.
>
> I myself am doing some work on the Tree of Life, and it is coming out serially in my little magazine. I should much value your opinion on it ... [11]

The work she was doing on the Tree of Life referred to her own impending classic *The Mystical Qabalah*, which came out in 1935. She was presumably excited by what she was reading in Regardie's proofs, because on 14 November 1932 she wrote to him again:

> . . . I suppose you know you have given away the old 'Golden Dawn' system, lock, stock and barrel? It is guarded by oaths with the most appalling penalties. I trust you have not been slain by

---

11. Personal collection of Maria Babwahsingh.

invisible forces! There will be some very angry folk in certain quarters. However, what you have said, badly wanted saying; I have done a certain amount myself in that direction not as much as you have. You have made my discrete [*sic*] contributions look like the day after the fair!

I hope the opportunity for us to meet will occur in the not too remote future.

They met up the next day. There followed another letter from her dated 16 November 1932, showing that they had pulled out all stops to meet.

I am so glad you liked us, because we liked you! I hope your visit will be the first of many, for there are many interesting things we could discuss together. I do so much laying down of the law to those who simply sit at my feet and open their mouths that it is a great pleasure to meet someone to whom I can talk 'on the level'.

It would be very interesting if we could do some practical work together; the equipment and the conditions are here for the undertaking. We must meet again in the near future and discuss possibilities . . .

No, I had no thought whatever of spying in connection with you, and I hope that you had none in connection with my interest in A.C., for whom I have a sneaking regard. I wish one could do something for him without burning one's fingers over him.

So she had clearly not yet met the Beast by this time, and was keen to question Regardie about him, as would anyone. When *The Mystical Qabalah* came out, she stated quite clearly that while she drew upon the writings of MacGregor Mathers and Aleister Crowley, she had never known either of them personally. Mathers had died in 1919, and Crowley—well, although she did not say it, was not the sort of individual a respectable married woman would try to track down. As he was living in England by this time, and would do for the rest of his life, he is more likely to have become aware of her emergence as a figure of importance in the strange world of Magick and made tentative overtures toward her—especially after seeing her praise of his own writings. An example of this is found in her essay 'Ceremonial Magic Unveiled' when she writes in a way that would make Crowley's ears prick up, and his ego purr with delight:

> In a hundred years' time, when the controversies concerning his personality have died down, Crowley will be recognised, quite apart from his occult work, as a great English writer of both prose and poetry . . . Although Crowley's writings are marred by the grossest ribaldry and the foulest personal abuse, they are the works of a man of genius and a writer of magnificent English . . .[12]

She was right and wrong. Although he wrote some magickal works of fractured genius, he was never a great English writer. His poetry, except for some gems, has not stood the test of time, and his fiction is banal. Everyone approaches *Moonchild* for the first time with an air of excitement about the unusual subject matter, and most come away disappointed with the ineptness of style and banal characterisation. There is not even any deep or unexpected magick buried between the lines to exercise the senses, and it is easy to glimpse Crowley the Poseur, with his chin up and chest out, pontificating to his captive audience and telling them how marvellous he is. In its day it might have been seen as avant-garde prose, but now it is frankly turgid. Compare it with Dion Fortune's *Moon Magic*, and it is quite obvious that in that genre at least she was in a far higher league as a writer. Whether either of them knew it or not is another matter.

She went on to say:

> To speak any word in mitigation of the general condemnation of Crowley is a thankless task, for panic-stricken people immediately conclude that one is in league with the devil. Nevertheless Mr. Re-

---

12. This essay appears on the Society of the Inner Light's website, at www .innerlight.org.uk/journals/Vol24No1/cermagic.htm (accessed 5 August 2009).

gardie has had the courage to do this, and I should like to add my voice to his.

If ever Mr Crowley, wandering in the wastes, had wanted an ally who would value him for his sheer dedication to Magick, and not care too much about the public persona, then she was there, in 3QT, willing to stand on the wall and take shots from all directions.

DF's contact with Regardie, however, went on to have explosive consequences, for she sponsored his admission into the Hermes Temple of the Golden Dawn, which was run by Hope Hughes and Ada Severs, described by Christine Hartley as 'those two silly women'. They were described as silly women by quite a number of others because, after he had attained the grade of Theoricus Adeptus Minor, he left the Order in December of 1934 and promptly published all the Knowledge Papers which they had entrusted to him. They were not the only ones to find him enchanting, however. Maiya Tranchell Hayes, in a letter to Jane Wolfe, commented: 'I frequently hear from Israel Regardie who is always charming. I lend him papers as he wants them—he is a really hard worker, full of knowledge'.[13]

Because of all this publication it was felt by some that the very existence of the Golden Dawn was now in peril, although as Regardie himself disarmingly pointed out, publication of the Roman Catholic Mass had not damaged Christianity one bit.

Dion, who felt some responsibility for sponsoring his entry into the Hermes Temple, took his side in the dispute. After all, she had also been accused of breaking her oaths with the books she had done. Five years before she had already stepped into the controversy with some very forthright remarks in 'Ceremonial Magic Unveiled', in which she defended Regardie's decision to publish his own first two books that had derived from the same source:

---

13. O. T. O. archives, 17 July 1934.

There is no legitimate reason that I have ever been able to see for keeping these things secret. If they have any value as an aid to spiritual development, and I for one believe that they have the highest value, there can be no justification for withholding them from the world...

Whatever other things that might have been levelled at her, no one has ever doubted that she had the 'welfare of humanity' at her very heart. As for the relationship between Dion Fortune and Israel Regardie, they seem to have fallen out, as usually happens between strong-willed magicians. In a letter dated 11 June 1938, she finished coolly with: 'I cannot see my way to be of any assistance to you in the matter as the controversy is one in which I do not care to be involved. I may say, however, that the reference to myself is without foundation. So far as I am aware, I have no occasion to complain of your behaviour to me personally, though I think you have treated some of my friends very badly'.[14]

The year 1935 saw the publication of *The Mystical Qabalah*, which was something of a highlight in Dion's career as a magical writer. She followed that with her novels *The Goat-Foot God*, *The Sea Priestess*, and *Moon Magic*, although *Moon Magic* was not published until ten years after her death. As she herself commented, with increasing confidence, her *Mystical Qabalah* gives the reader all the theories they might need, but the novels give the actual practice, and between them it was like receiving the keys of the Temple.

She was right to be proud of the book. It is clear, it is deep, and it came to influence almost all of the later books on what might be termed the Qabalah of the West. She took the best of Mathers, the relevant pieces from Crowley, and used her own formidable intuition plus her well-crafted writing ability to make this most arcane of top-

---

14. Personal collection of Maria Babwahsingh.

ics accessible. You have to know a very great deal about a topic, and be completely imbued with it, in order to write simply and lucidly so that the ordinary man or woman in the street can understand it, and this she manages admirably.

But from Crowley's side of the caduceus, 1935 also saw him humiliated in the courts and declared bankrupt. This came a year after trying to sue Nina Hamnett for libel following some fairly innocuous comments in her book *The Laughing Torso*. Sadly, it was Crowley the Man who was seen in court, and the Magus was nowhere in sight. By every account except his own, he was seen as cutting a rather pitiful figure, his attempts at witty, cutting sallies coming somewhere between a second-rate Oscar Wilde and a third-rate Winston Churchill. Today, the state of bankruptcy can be seen as something of a badge of honour, or a mere hiatus in the normal progress of life, but it was a major scandal then. And yet Crowley did what Crowley had always done . . . he just sort of shrugged and kept on.

However, if his performance before the court under cross-examination won him no admirers, as he was leaving the court a woman named Patricia MacAlpine (whom he came to call 'Deidre') approached him and offered to have his child. Nine months later his first and only son, Aleister Ataturk, was born.

In fact, although he was by now approaching sixty, and not in the best physical shape, a heroin addict and severe asthmatic, to the astonishment of many presumably envious folk he maintained a constant stream of lovers, male and female, right up to the end of his life.

What did he look like then?

Viola Bankes was not an occultist, but she had once acted as the middleman between Crowley and the black actor, Paul Robeson, in the—unsuccessful—attempt to get Robeson to play a leading role in

Crowley's play, *Mortadello*. For years, she wrote, the name of Aleister Crowley had excited her in the same way that all Europe in the eighteenth century was excited by Cagliostro. When she finally met him her impressions were thus:

> He had neither the powerful compelling features of a magician nor the strong and nervous hands of a poet. His hands were unusually small and well-kept, and reminded me of a delicate bird's claws; rapacious, perhaps, but not masterful. His voice, which I had imagined would be sonorous, was light and rather high for a man. In his eyes, however, lay the answer to the riddle. There was no doubt that this man, with his colossal will-power and deep occult knowledge, could dominate a weaker and untrained will to the extent that is called magnetism, and could, if he wished, obtain absolute mastery over the mind and body of his subject . . . . In repose, the eyes held the sleepy reserve of the Oriental, but when he opened them wide and deliberately fastened them on another person, that person could scarcely fail to feel the thrill of magnetism that emanated from their green depths.[15]

Another who was struck by Crowley's magnetism was Bernard Bromage, who felt that he was a hypnotist of no mean order, adding: 'I could credit some of the tales I had heard of his immense fascination for women; how, granted the time and the date and the loved one all together, they would surrender all they had, money, titles, social position, to take up their burden and follow him!'[16]

⁓

As for DF at the same time, Ithell Colquhoun described how she went to one of the public lectures that were given in the large drawing room on an upper floor of 3QT:

---

15. Viola Bankes, *Why Not?* (London: Jarrolds Publishers, 1934).
16. *Light* magazine (published by the College of Psychic Studies), vol. LXXIX, 1959.

I remember going to one in 1934 when her husband took the chair. She was a big woman simply and conventionally dressed with faded blond hair, who might at first glance have passed for a headmistress or matron of a nursing home. Only her eyes, deep blue and glittering, suggested something less easily accepted. I forget the title of her discourse but I remember the sturdy common-sense of her approach—outwardly at least—and her warning against the bogus Orders, the sharks and the charlatans of London's occult world. She was vigorous and well-spoken, possessed of a certain degree of hypnotic power—sometime used, if current rumour did not lie, to extract donations from her disciples for the benefit of her Fraternity, of course.[17]

While the latter comment was certainly pure nonsense, it shows how even someone as apparently squeaky-clean as Dion Fortune could attract rather scurrilous and unnecessary asides. So imagine the sort of venom that the Great Beast would drawn down upon himself without even trying.

On the other hand, she was not perhaps as pure as some of her contemporaries hoped. Remember that the Hermes Temple was supposed to have fallen out with DF when it was reported to Hope Hughes that she had been doing a black magic rite with a naked woman within the FIL. This was either a case of Dion pulling someone's leg, which she was not averse to doing, or one of the more delicate members of Hermes catching a glimpse of one of the 'polarity rites' that seemed to feature in the higher levels of the lodge.

During this period Crowley had a number of Scarlet Women, which we will define later, all of whom were expected to have a certain level of appealingly appalling sexual behaviour. It might be supposed that the happily married pillar of respectability Mrs Violet

---

17. Ithell Colquhoun, *The Sword of Wisdom*.

Evans would be far removed from that sort of thing, and yet it was just as necessary for her own Work that she had her priests.

As her own inner Master explained, via trance communications:

> You can get exchange of magnetism between two of the same sex, but the trouble is that the flow thus exchanged cannot flow in circuit . . .
>
> In the days when her husband [Penry Evans] afforded her some protection there were no difficulties, but now the protection is withdrawn the group must afford her it. She must be able to work thus without being exposed to scandalous tongues . . . [18]

During this period the known priests she worked with were Thomas Penry Evans, her husband; C. T. Loveday, the loyal co-founder of her lodge; Lt Colonel Charles 'Kim' Seymour; and, toward the end of this period, W. K. Creasy. The Master also implied that there had been others, not generally known about.

She was also greatly taken at this time with the character and writings of Bernard Bromage, author of *The Occult Arts of Ancient Egypt* and *The Secret Rites of Tibetan Yoga*—a man well-versed in anything tantric. But before he met Dion Fortune he had made a number of visits to the Great Beast, and had come away rather irritated by his antics:

> [I] listened politely while Crowley walked round me studying me from all angles. Among other antics he did a breathing exercise down the back of my neck. (The way he did this testified to some knowledge of the Tantric hypnotic system with which I happen to be more familiar than most; more familiar, in fact, than was Crowley. So I was able to counter this move with a little astral dexterity of my own devising; and the Master retreated to the curtained window!)[19]

---

18. Gareth Knight, *Dion Fortune and the Inner Light*, p. 262.
19. *Light* magazine, vol. LXXIX, 1959.

Yet he acknowledged that the old mage had a great knowledge of the Hindu and Tibetan Tantras, the relation of the Kabbalah to the Sanskrit magical system, Egyptian occult rites, and modern alchemy. He also obviously knew a great deal about the Oriental approach to 'the sex question', as they tended to call it then.

Later on when Bromage made a very warm acquaintance with Dion Fortune he was impressed by her in-depth knowledge and practical experience of modern psychology, and saw that she had discerned for herself the connection between modern empiricism and the tried and tested tenets of the great tantric and Qabalistic ritualists.

> I recall many discussions with her on these and kindred topics: on the nature of the love technique and how it is the woman, the positive dynamism, who awakens the energy in the male and so makes him positive; of the part played by the ancestral subconscious in the formation of character and personality; of the tremendous and sometimes terrifying power of suggestion and its use in propaganda; of the nature of the child and the perception of animals.[20]

This was all clearly an outer expression of work that she had been doing privately for some time. In simple terms, when it came to the subtleties of polarity workings, she was not merely speculating: she knew her stuff inside out.

Although one of her most influential priests, Seymour, broke away from the FIL and continued to work with Christine Hartley, he left behind a legacy of superb essays, including the manual of self-initiation called 'The Old Religion'. Hartley pointed out to the present writer that in essence *all* magic is sex magic—though not necessarily on the physical plane. Insisting that she and Seymour had never been lovers, she added: 'But that does not mean that sex was not involved'. Instead there was an interchange of energies on magical levels for which physical

---

20. *Light* magazine, Spring 1960.

intercourse is but a lower analogue. As Seymour wrote in his Magical Diaries for this period: 'I *drove* the energy over to her. And she *drew* it from me'.[21]

The Great Beast would have had no time for that approach. He would have been all over any priestess that got within range. As Alan Adams pointed out though, Crowley couldn't tell the difference between a priestess and a whore.[22]

But, of course, the pressing thing in all their lives just then were the events in Europe and the storm clouds that were so obviously gathering, summoned up by the strong, self-styled god-men who were now ruling Italy and Germany. Make no mistake, everyone in the early 1930s had a fascination for the emerging fascist regimes there, although Crowley claimed dismissively to have 'seen through' Mussolini ten years earlier, shortly after his rise to power. The fact that Il Duce had had him expelled from Italy might have played some small part in that, however.

On the other hand, a number of the English upper classes in particular were mightily drawn toward this new phenomenon of Nazism—particularly King Edward VIII. When he abdicated in 1936 it was little to do with his love for Mrs Wallis Simpson triumphing over the staid mores of the British Establishment. That was just a front. The British government affected outrage at his affair with a married woman because they knew he had been selling high-grade military secrets to the Nazis for some time, and was, in every meaning of the word, a traitor. By trotting out the Archbishop of Canterbury and the like to express concern and distaste, and thus precipitating the abdication, it helped

---

21. Alan Richardson, 20*th* Century Magic and the Old Religion: Dion Fortune, Christine Hartley, Charles Seymour (St. Paul, MN: Llewellyn, 1991).

22. Charles Fielding and Carr Collins, *The Story of Dion Fortune*.

the government avoid the possibility that they might one day have to consider hanging their king-emperor for high treason.

In the early days of Hitler's rise to power, neither Crowley nor Fortune would have known quite what to make of the Führer, although the ageing Beast, with an eye for the main chance as always, wrote to George Viereck in 1936:

> Hitler himself says emphatically in *Mein Kampf* that the world needs a new religion, that he himself is not a religious teacher, but that when the proper man appears he will be welcome.[23]

Needless to say, Crowley was quite certain that the Proper Man concerned was himself. In the event, the Nazi Party proved totally inimical to the O.T.O., arresting Karl Germer and suppressing anything and anyone remotely challenging to their authority. If Crowley felt that Hitler's aims in *Mein Kampf* were in some sense inspired—perhaps wrongly—by the *Book of the Law* that he had channelled some thirty years before, he rather hoped to see some tangible recognition at the highest levels, whether it was via the British aristocracy or the Nazi leaders that so many of them admired.

And this is the essence of Aleister Crowley: he associated himself fully with the great gods and the international events that were unfolding at that time, and there was never a point in which he thought, This is nothing to do with little me .... When, in his rites, he 'Assumed the God Form' in order to identify with and thus channel the appropriate god-consciousness, he never really came back to earth afterward.

Dion Fortune, in contrast, never lost sight of the fact that after 'rising on the planes' to the highest levels of mystical awareness and union with the Goddess, that she had to come back down to earth afterward,

---

23. Quoted in Lawrence Sutin, *Do What Thou Wilt*, from the O.T.O. archives.

and function as simple Mrs Evans, with a home to run and relationships to nurture, and so she never really lost herself.

So what events and influences would have conspired to make them
so different, and yet so similar?

For that we have to move to 1920, and the crucial happenings in
both their lives.

chapter four

TEMPLES AND THEIR TRUTHS

In 1920 Aleister Crowley fathered two children by two supportive women, Leah Hirsig and Ninette Shumway, who already had small boys from previous relationships. After consulting the I Ching—which he did throughout his life—he decided that he would move the whole brood to a small medieval town on the northern coast of Sicily. And so the Abbey of Thelema was founded in Cefalu, from where he planned to spread the Word of the Aeon. The name was borrowed from the satire by François Rabelais,[1] *Gargantua and Pantagruel*, where the Abbey of Theleme was described as a sort of anti-monastery, wherein which the inhabitants' lives were 'spent not in laws, statutes, or rules, but according to their own free will and pleasure'.

Although the I Ching's influence on Crowley's decision making should not be minimised, Richard Spence's study of French, German, and Italian intelligence archives found that he was as likely to have been sent to Cefalu by his superiors to spy on Italian naval movements, as well as keep an eye on activities in nearby French-controlled Tunisia. It does seem certain, though, that these same superiors in London by now had grave reservations about Crowley's chronic inability to manage money, as well as his 'moral corruption'.

---

1. 1494–1553.

Nevertheless, Crowley rented a solidly built one-story farmhouse with thick walls and a tiled roof that to mortals had been known as the Villa Santa Barbara, but which he promptly re-antichristened the 'Collegium ad Spiritum Sanctum'. This grandly named establishment consisted of five rooms off a central chamber which became the actual temple, in the centre of which stood a six-sided altar, and on which were kept six candles and the traditional magickal 'Weapons' of sword, wand, cup, and shield, plus the all-important *Book of the Law*. By the following year the other rooms were all decorated according to the tastes of Crowley the Artist, including 'La Chambre des Cauchemars', or Room of Nightmares, the walls of which were covered in poetry, prophecy, and graphic examples of every kind of sexuality his graphically sexual mind could envision.

Every morning he would invoke Ra, at noon Hathor, at dusk it was Tum, finally Kheper at midnight. He gave frequent services in the temple and performed his own Gnostic Mass. The men and women wore blue robes, with hoods. There was nude sunbathing. There was a lot of sexual activity. In fact, the Master and his holy whores acted out every intense urge and impulse his astonishing imagination and demanding libido could devise. He insisted that this was never for mere human gratification, but as part of a calculated magickal progress designed to purify and perfect the soul.

Newcomers had an initial introductory period of three days of gracious treatment. If they decided to stay on, then they faced a curriculum that was scheduled to last three months, during which they would follow the teachings of Crowley's A. A., as well taking lessons in yoga and basic ritual magick, studying Crowley's already voluminous writings, and learning to rise on the planes—usually with the help of drugs. They had to record everything in a personal diary which was left available for others to read, thus generally baring their souls to all and sundry. Plus they had to fulfil those obligations needed for the Abbey to function successfully: shopping, cooking, cleaning, and acting as the Master's secretary when required.

The compulsory study curriculum included four classes of books, A–D, with Class A consisting of certain tomes which represented: '... the utterance of an Adept entirely beyond the criticism of even the Visible Head of the Organization'. This meant all of the Master's books, of course, and instead of being a statement of incredible pomposity, this was probably Crowley giving one of his (frequently misunderstood or not even perceived) sly winks at the world.

This section also included: *Liber* I, which was an account of the Grade of Magus; *Liber* VII, which had seven chapters referring to the seven planets of Mars, Saturn, Jupiter, Sol, Mercury, Luna, and Venus; *Liber* X, which was about '... the sending forth of the Master by the A..A.. and an explanation of his mission'; *Liber* XXVII, '... being a book of Trigrams of the Mutations of the TAO with the YIN and the YANG'.

And many many more, but with especial reference to his masterpiece *Liber* CCXX, also known as *Liber al vel Legis*, which was '... the foundation of the New Aeon, and thus of the whole of our Work'.

In other words, the *Book of the Law*, of which more later.

Disciples came, studied, and went. A few spoke highly of their experiences there, and embraced the climate of sexual anything-goes. Others were frankly appalled by the sheer filth, though by this they meant the actual physical dirtiness of the place. If it might have been a gleaming temple in the astral light to the illuminated gaze of the Master, it was anything but that to the earthly eyes of some would-be disciples. Then again, many of them came from the sort of wealthy backgrounds which would regard any kind of rustic existence as intrinsically dirty.

Sadly, exasperatingly, the Abbey came to resemble the worst sort of smashed-out, stoned-witless, free-loving drug squat of the later hippy era which came to venerate Crowley. Whatever gratuitous grace they felt was being bestowed upon them inwardly, by opiates, was not reflected on the outer planes. The endless supply of drugs, randomly administered—sometimes without the disciple know-ing—meant that some individuals never quite recovered. The Master Therion in particular. Crowley had sniffed, ingested, and smoked his way through the realms of hashish, anhalonium, ether, and mesca-line without, he felt, these seriously touching him or dampening his Will. But cocaine and heroin sucked him down and down, into the horrible hole from which he never quite emerged. At this time he was taking three grains of heroin a day; at the end of his life he needed eleven. It was to his shame that he, a Priest of Horus—the Priest of the Aeon who had driven off Abra-melin demons and the soul-devouring Choronzon—could not master heroin and cocaine.

What would Dion Fortune make of this particular aspect? Well, she was fully aware of the virtues that might have resulted from the GD training in ritual magic, as modified for the A. A. In her experi-ence the adepts of the Golden Dawn, using purely psychic methods, were able to obtain far better results than could be obtained by users of hashish and mescal—without the disastrous after-effects.

In *Applied Magic* she expanded on this, clearly with Crowley in mind:

> The risk to which these drugs expose those who use them is psy-chic, not physical; they may, if the experimenter is not an expert oc-cultist, thoroughly competent in sealings and banishings, lay their user open to psychic invasion, and even obsession, because they open the doors of the astral to the unprepared consciousness . . .[2]

---

2. 'The Occult Field Today', from Dion Fortune, *Applied Magic*, p. 76.

Actually Crowley himself, after an experience of great spiritual bliss, once wondered how much of his attainment was due to his magical practices and how much to the hashish. Still high from both, he decided only 10 percent was due to the drug. Sometimes, you have to wonder what he might have achieved—if anything—if he had left the stuff alone.

So, Dion would never have lasted long at the Abbey. Despite that vague but rather naïve support for the use of certain drugs, Crowley would have damned her as a prude and slipped something into her food that would *really* get her chakras whirling, then (in his words) slapped her arse and buggered her in order to help her find her True Will.[3] Yet despite the hints of a high moral tone from Dion, and the tendency of any reader to sympathise with a wild maverick like the Beast, the younger mage was absolutely right when it came to her comments on drugs. Underneath, he knew this. In fact, he tried to find a sanatorium where he could direct his own medical treatment; otherwise he would have to admit that his theories had failed—or he had failed his Gods.

But amid all this apparent chaos, putative dirt, and apparent sexual degradation, Crowley's own comments must be borne in mind: 'My whole plan is to clean all germs out of the sexual wound ... My object is not merely to disgust but to root out ruthlessly the sense of sin'. He meant it. He meant it with all of his extraordinary heart and soul, as part of an ancient and honourable system whereby individuals would try to win through to purity and gnosis by confronting and indulging in all their darkest urges or fears. And whenever he had sex—which was often—it was *always* as part of the Magnum Opus, the attempt to achieve union with God, and never for mere gratification.

---

3. By all accounts, this was his preferred method of sexual congress with a woman. With men, he invariably took the passive role.

Some have said it actually worked. Others have disagreed, but hinted that they managed to have an awful lot of fun along the way, which is not always the case in this business of Magick.

⌒

And where was Dion Fortune at this time? Well, oddly enough she was also involved in magical work within an Abbey. This one had been in existence for over a thousand years, had been built, rebuilt, and expanded until it was, for a time, one of the jewels in medieval Christendom, and a pilgrimage centre par excellence. Although its outer structures were ruined by the time that Dion came there, its inner shape and function held true and eternal to her psychic vision. So instead of the hot climes of the Mediterranean, she was spending more and more time in the green and often damp west of England, obsessed with the Abbey of that small town that had once been called *Ynys Vitrin*, or Isle of Glass, and which was now known as Glastonbury. It was hereabouts in 1920–21 that she was developing her own powers of trance mediumship in collaboration with that important figure mentioned earlier, Maiya Tranchell Hayes, and—quite separately—Bligh Bond.

Actually at this time the former's name was Mabel Gertrude Webb,[4] wife of Dr John Curtis Webb, who wrote two books revolutionary for the time: *Electro-therapy in Gynaecology* and *Electro-therapy: Its Rationale and Indications*. They read fearsomely today, but what he tried to develop (and with some apparent success) was an early version of a TENS unit—a Transcutaneous Electrical Nerve Stimulator.

Mabel—for she had not yet become Maiya—acted as a kind of watcher to make sure the entranced Dion was not troubled by low-grade spirits. The whole process was carefully directed and supervised, and the communications checked and tested to see if they

---

4. There is a letter in the Warburg Institute from Mrs Curtis Webb to Norman Mudd, Crowley's most hard-wearing disciple, but access to it will not become available until 31 December 2039.

were genuine contacts with useful inner beings, rather than mere audible daydreams. All the communications that came through were later scrutinised in the light of Dion's knowledge of Freudian symbolism to see if any of them were the results of wish fulfilment by her own subconscious, and thus not to be trusted at all. The occult techniques being used were based upon those she had learned in the Golden Dawn.

At the autumn equinox of 1921, she and her mother Sarah Firth, and Frederick Bligh Bond, saw her mediumship make contact with an inner-plane group known as the Watchers of Avalon. Through them they learned about the College of Illuminati, which used to exist at Glastonbury. It described the unbroken line of descent of mystic power that connected directly with the elemental powers of the soil, in which are the roots of the soul of the race. They learned about the Sun worship and Serpent worship of the Northern Tribes, the power of the Abbey and the original wattle church founded by Joseph of Arimathea, the principles of Cosmic architecture, and the true nature of the Druids.

And they could hardly fail to learn about the great hill known as the Tor, less well-understood to the public but even more attractive, the breast of a vast and sleeping Goddess, the tower on top being a nipple filled with milk. On good days the energies from the underworld spume into the atmosphere with the sense of a fountain; on other days it radiates an air of near menace.

Around the two, said to be built into the landscape, were discerned huge figures portraying some primaeval zodiac. And it was in a little wooden chalet at the foot of the Tor, in the Chalice Orchard, that Dion found her most enduring home. For all the attractions of 3QT, despite the marvels worked there, it is the Chalice Orchard that people most associate with her, as the Abbey of the Aeon at Cefalu is inseparable from its founder.

Perhaps it was because here the Christian sense of duality was re-solved, for to the Druids of the Glass Isle good and bad, right and wrong, black and white, body and soul were quite unknown. The key to the Celtic philosophy was the merging of dark and light, natural and supernatural, conscious and unconscious. To her mind there were three roads to Glastonbury: the high road of history, the upland path of legend, and the secret Green Road of the soul. On the other hand she could also get there by courtesy of the Great Western Rail-way, and be within the 'holyest earthe in England' within a few hours. Here she put down a psychic tendril into the depths and rooted her-self for all time. Whatever Crowley might have been doing on the in-ner planes in the Chamber of Nightmares for individuals, Dion For-tune used her little place at Glastonbury to open up the 'secret Green Road' into those parallel, maddening, enchanting, and very powerful dimensions of Faery for the generations that followed.[5]

At that time, too, in the early 1920s, the Master Therion was rather looking to find a successful pupil—one who would learn all that he had to teach, prove a shining example of his creed, and then go on to tell the world: A*d majorem Crowley gloriam*,[6] so to speak. It was in late 1922 that he felt he had found the perfect disciple—and that is not too strong a term—in the shape of Frederick Charles Loveday, an Ox-ford graduate of some distinction, who preferred to be called Raoul.

Raoul and his wife, Betty May, arrived at the Abbey in Novem-ber 1922, and Crowley felt at once that his pupil—whom he called Frater Aud—would make staggering magickal progress under his guidance. Despite his wife's detestation of the whole regime, Love-day worked right hard under the supervision of what he regarded as

---

5. See Alan Richardson, *Priestess: The Life and Magic of Dion Fortune*, revised and ex-panded edition (Loughborough, UK: Thoth Publications, 2007). All future refer-ences are to this version only.

6. 'To the greater glory of Crowley'.

a living Master. There were no wonders of the obvious sort, except mysterious blue lights and visions of a bull-deity, but then Crowley once said that while he as Magus may have lacked power, he did have the ability to precipitate spiritual crises within people, which he felt was part of his role as Prophet of the Aeon. Unfortunately Raoul's crisis was an entirely physical one, for he contracted acute enteric fever precipitated by drinking from a polluted mountain spring, and so the potential Magical Son died—stillborn, so to speak—in February 1923.

In that same period, along with those early beginnings of her work in Glastonbury, Dion was deeply involved in a very similar magical curriculum to that which should have been experienced in Cefalu, but this was organised by her own teacher, the Irishman Theodore Moriarty (1873–1923), and run from the sun-washed suburbs of Bishop's Stortford, in Hertfordshire. This one, however, was entirely free of sex and drugs, though the leader did tend to smoke like a chimney.

If a primary requirement of all gurus is the ability to attract people willing to finance their spirituality, then Dr Moriarty was no exception. His own occult 'college' was made possible through the support of three sisters: Gwen Stafford-Allen, Elsie Reeves, and Ursula Allen-Williams, plus a couple of dozen followers, including the young and somewhat unpopular Violet Firth, who was beginning to make a pen-name for herself with the short stories she wrote for *Royal* magazine as Dion Fortune—the first appearance of that name in print.

It was from Gwen's large house The Grange that they ran the genteel-sounding Science, Arts and Craft Society, with the Irishman as the presiding genius. He insisted they call him Doctor, rather than Master as some of them wanted to do, though in fact he had neither a medical degree nor a PhD from any traceable source.[7]

---

7. For further details, see *Priestess: The Life and Magic of Dion Fortune*. Thoth edition only.

Moriarty was never an initiate of the Golden Dawn, but came to his ceremonial via Freemasonry, espousing along the way a sort of 'Universal Theosophy', though there are no records of him ever having been a member there. Moriarty sought permission from his Masonic lodge to admit and initiate women, organising it all himself, and keeping it independent of any of the Co-Masonic groups. And what he taught—and which became so important to Dion—was the wisdom of lost Atlantis. Especially that deriving from what he described as the sacerdotal college in the city of Glwn ('sometimes called Glaun', as Moriarty wrote somewhat schoolmasterishly), which lay along the banks of the mighty river Naradek.

According to his own vision, the essence of the Atlantean teaching had been brought down through the ages by the likes of Horus, Mithras, Quetzalcoatl, and Buddha. Each epoch produced an exemplar of the Christos Principle, whose task it was to manifest a state of consciousness just ahead of the prevailing human consciousness of that epoch. Crowley would have added the Master Therion to that list, because of course that is exactly how he saw himself, though he seems to have shown little interest in Atlantis—if indeed he ever believed in its physical existence in the first place.

Like the Abbey on Cefalu, Moriarty organised his occult college along what are now called Gurdjieffian lines, after the work done by the Armenian mystic George Ivanovich Gurdjieff at Fontainebleau near Paris.[8] That is to say pupils were made to labour in areas that were not natural to them or easy. Intellectuals were given hard and mindless physical tasks; the more rugged sort were given secretarial duties. There was constant challenge and fierce discipline, and a certain amount of private debate as to whether that sort of thing had any benefit whatsoever. The programme was also continued in Sinclair Road, Hammersmith, in London, but most notably in deepest Hamp-

---

8. There is evidence to suggest that Gurdjieff was really a Cockney orphan named Frederick Dottle.

shire between 1920 and 1922, in The Orchard, Eversley, owned by
Gwen's sister, Elsie Reeves.

The events at Crowley's Abbey of Thelema were more notable at
the time for the drug and sexual excesses therein than for the inner
work that was attempted. But the entirely chaste and drug-free do-
ings in The Orchard still have the power to fascinate today, largely
because of Dion's odd autobiography, *Psychic Self-Defence*, which was
published in the same year that saw Crowley's *Confessions* appear, and
dealt largely with the extraordinary events surrounding her years in
the early 1920s with her very own Dr Mirabilis.

Of course she would have been entirely aware of those outrageous
outer events in Cefalu because once the widowed Betty May was back
in England she told the *Sunday Express* all about her time with the Great
Beast, and blamed him completely for Raoul's death. If Crowley had
never had his wicked way with Betty—purely for magickal reasons of
course—then she now did her best to shaft him completely.

All this notoriety had a knock-on effect with the Italian government under Mussolini, which had become twitchy about any kind
of secret society, starting with the Freemasons, and which decided
they wanted this devil-worshipper out of their country as quickly as
possible. To Crowley's astonishment, they served an expulsion order
on him by April. Crowley, who by this time felt he had achieved the
magical grade of Ipsissimus, and thus was free from all mortal limita-
tions and necessity, living in perfect balance with the manifest universe, once again became a wanderer in the wastes.

And as the death of Raoul Loveday was being reported in the popular press, Dion was herself involved with a Loveday, though this one
was no academic genius, and there had never been a suggestion of
anything remotely improper between them.

~

Charles Thomas Loveday, whose Magical Name or motto was Amor
Vincit Omnia—love conquers all—was sixteen years older than Dion

Fortune, and held a senior position with London Tramways. The two Lovedays do not seem to have been related. Dion and Charles met on a moonlit night at Chalice Well, on the edges of Glastonbury, and although they never became lovers he remained devoted to her for the rest of her life, and is buried a few feet away from her.

While Raoul had been hoping to explore and perfect his own Paganism, the very gentle Frater AVO was keen on founding The Guild of the Master Jesus in 1923. Although good and perhaps great things seem to have been achieved within Loveday's Guild over time, it became something of an outer court for the Community of the Inner Light, founded the following year, which in turn developed into the full-blown magical lodge known as the Fraternity of the Inner Light, founded in 1927 when DF felt that she had magical status, experience, and inner contacts to enable her to do so. Some of the senior magicians in the FIL wrote the Guild off as a dumping ground because they saw that real heavy-duty magical work was being done in both 3QT in London and Chalice Orchard in Glastonbury.

The curriculum of her magical lodge involved study of her own channelled book *The Cosmic Doctrine*, her own take on the Kabbalah as learned within the Golden Dawn, plus intensive individual and group ritual work using the archetypes of Avalon—of King Arthur, Morgan le Fay, and Merlin; the strange Celtic Saints; the Holy Grail and Holy Thorn; the faery worlds of the Sidhe which intermingle with ours; and the Old Gods and Goddesses of Britain which preceded everything Christian and Druidic, and which may have had Atlantean forebears that came there after the cataclysm.

Dion worked with the Native British and purely Western deities at this phase in her magic, and she managed to make them universal in their relevance. Anyone in America or Australia, for example, could make valid inner contacts with the archetypes of Britain—which is perhaps better seen as a strata of consciousness within the psyche rather than a geopolitical entity. Before her, very few magicians had really given much thought to working with the Celtic and pre-Celtic deities of Keridwen, Arianrhod, Branwen, or the Morrigan and the like;[9] now, they seem to be everywhere.

Crowley, despite references to the Graal, or Holy Grail, worked almost exclusively with all those Mystery Cults surrounding the Mediterranean, making best use of his formidable Classical scholarship, and seemingly not aware or not interested in the traditions of his own land. Nevertheless, he likewise showed that an aspirant in England could effectively work with the deities of Greece or Egypt without having any need to go to those countries.

They were both of them writing furiously at this time. In 1922 Dion began that series of short stories collectively called *The Secrets of Dr Taverner*, stories which were published in *Royal* magazine and based firmly upon Moriarty, who was still living.

Crowley meanwhile, when not working on his brilliant *Confessions*, wrote the populist *Diary of a Drug Fiend* in a deliberate and quite reasonable attempt to cash in on what he saw as the public hysteria and prurience attached to the subject of the drug traffic. Not only was the £60 advance a lifeline for the cash-strapped Beast, he saw it as a confirmation on the spiritual plane of their work on behalf of the New Aeon, and sought to show that drug addiction could be dealt with by exercising the True Will.

In fact, by this time the World Teacher of this same New Aeon had found the one Master to whom he would always defer, bow, and often cringe for the rest of his life, and it was called heroin; and all the magick in all the worlds was unable to free him of his addiction, Logos or not.

However, by describing himself as the World Teacher of the New Aeon, as he did in his book of this period called *The Heart of the Master*,

---

9. W. B. Yeats was a notable exception.

he was having a dig at something that irritated him a little, but which troubled Dion Fortune very much indeed: he was taking a swipe at that young Indian boy being hailed across the civilised world as a Messiah in all but name.

~

Jiddhu Krishnamurti (1895–1986) was effectively adopted by the prominent occultist and leading Theosophist Charles Webster Leadbeater, who had seen the boy as a 'vehicle' for the eagerly anticipated World Teacher. In other words, another version of the Logos theme.

With the avid support of Annie Besant, who was the head of the Theosophical Society at that time, they created the 'Order of the Star', which would foster his progress, spread his message, and generally seek to prepare the whole planet for the time when Krishnaji, as his intimates called him, uttered the Word that would announce His manifestation.

The fiercely misogynistic and thoroughly dreadful 'Bishop' Leadbeater had been described by both Crowley *and* Fortune as a Black Magician. Possessed of undoubted clairvoyance, supported by his devious and over-spiritualised ego, he completely dominated poor Mrs Besant, who had once been such an inspirational figure on the political scene, and a champion of oppressed women workers. A pederast, whom Krishnamurti would one day describe simply as being 'evil', Leadbeater somehow managed to survive the increasing scandals about his sexual activities.[10]

It is easy to see why Crowley never felt the need to waste too much spleen on the Order of the Star: he knew within his very bones, within every blood cell of his body, that *he*, the Master Therion, was the World Teacher, and not some insignificant little boy from the Indian subcontinent.

---

10. Gregory Tillett, *The Elder Brother: A Biography of Charles Webster Leadbeater* (London: Routledge & Kegan Paul Books, 1982).

In fact, he had had experience of Leadbeater and his compatriot James Wedgwood as early as 1913, when the Co-Masonic Order which they ran had shown interest in buying the Antient and Primitive Rite from John Yarker, and planned to turn it into a vehicle for the worship of the 'Alcyone', as Krishnamurti was known to the cognoscenti. At a meeting held in Manchester, Crowley verbally attacked Mrs Besant, described her as 'the nominal mistress' of the Theosophical Society, and her occult partner C. W. Leadbeater as a senile sex maniac, who was 'the hand which moves the wooden-headed pawn Wedgwood, hardly a man, certainly no Mason'.[11]

Dion, however, who had no exalted ideas about her own status, was quite certain that Leadbeater and his cronies (who seemed like beacons of light to the dear old ladies of the TS) were actually Black Magicians of the worst kind. She was greatly worried by this whole messianic movement, and found herself under psychic attack from one of the cohorts for being so outspoken.

Her psychic attacker was Bomanji Pestonji Wadia (1881–1958), who had come to England sometime around 1919 with the intent of founding an occult school of his own, one which would rival the work being accomplished by Leadbeater. Nowadays the fact that he was an Indian nationalist and wanted nothing better than to get the imperial British out of his country, is entirely understandable. Then, to someone like Dion, it made him an immediate object of suspicion. In fact she went to one of his meetings where, through meditative means, a small group of them were put in touch with the Himalayan Masters.

---

11. 'Report of the Proceedings at Manchester, with a Note on the Circumstances Which Led Up to Them' in *The Equinox*, September 1913, p. xxvii. Available online at http://www.the-equinox.org/vol1/no10/eqi10000.html (accessed 5 August 2009).

For what my testimony is worth, I can vouch for the genuineness of these contacts; I certainly got in touch with something; but although it was not evil, it was to me alien and unsympathetic, and it seemed to me that it was hostile to my race, but that is another story. Anyway the rapport came to an end so far as I was concerned. Whether I was cast out or walked out, I cannot be certain, anyway, the parting was simultaneous and by mutual agreement.[12]

To her dismay, as she had looked around at the little group, Dion felt that she was the only pure-blooded Anglo-Saxon present, and so took issue with Wadia over his idea that he would pour the regenerative spiritual force of the East into the group-soul of the British Empire, which *he* felt was in a very bad way indeed, but which *she* insisted was only tired by the war.

To Dion, who had never been outside her own country, the Himalayan peaks were places of mystery and enchantment, soaked with the sort of myths and legends which were like soul-food to some, and she had been brought up on all those tales of the Eastern Masters such as Koot Hoomi and Morya, which had provided so much of the energy behind the early Theosophical Society.

In sharp contrast, Aleister Crowley, the Wanderer in the Wastes who had rarely stayed in his own country, had successfully climbed some of the highest peaks in the Himalayas before any other mountaineer, had sexual relationships with men and women the length and breadth of the Indian subcontinent, lived as a Yogi, dressed as an Indian prince, eaten the food and drank the wine and ingested the drugs of that—to him—very real realm.

Nevertheless, it seemed to Dion that on very subtle levels her own nation was at risk from this guru named Wadia, and it was no surprise when she became subjected to a series of psychic onslaughts from him.

12. Quoted in O. E. [Oriental Esoteric] *Library Critic*.

One evening, as she sat chatting to a friend, she perceived his form within an egg-shaped sphere of misty light, and countered by attacking it using the sign of the pentagram and certain Names of Power, which drove it away. Nevertheless a sinister atmosphere remained, and her first response was to summon up her own Masters in the inner planes—Masters who were entirely Western, and likely to understand her concerns. The reply came back quite clearly that she was to contact a certain Colonel Fuller, who would attend her next lecture.

Now, Colonel J. F. C. 'Boney' Fuller was a figure of increasing eminence. Later on he became one of the only two Englishmen to be invited to Adolf Hitler's birthday party, and a close associate of Oswald Mosley, head of the British fascists, but he was also a genius in the art of warfare, with a profound knowledge of Magick. In fact, not too many years earlier, the Great Beast had had as many hopes for him as he had recently nurtured for Raoul.

To her surprise he did indeed appear, as he had had an inner voice of his own telling him that Dion was about to come and ask his help, and that he was to give it. Quite what he did she never knew, but a few days later Wadia left the country.

In the event, Dion's worries about the Order of the Star and Crowley's ire about Krishnamurti as a rival were later resolved not by magical battles or political manoeuvring, but by the young Vehicle himself. In 1929, to the astonishment of everyone and his own eternal credit, he dissolved the whole frantic, sordid structure that had built up around him, declaring the Truth was a pathless land, claiming no allegiance to any nationality, caste, religion, or philosophy, and spent the rest of his long life travelling the world as an individual, speaking to large and small groups and refusing any mantle.

Dion would have been impressed by such forthright honesty and courage. The Master Therion might have raised an unsurprised eyebrow.

Today, no one reveres Krishnamurti except as a dignified human; not many have heard of Dion Fortune; but many thousands across the world still regard Crowley as *the* Logos of the Aeon.

Ironically, this was made possible because of an organisation that sought to advance Crowley in a similar way to the Order of the Star's promotion of Krishnamurti—and for the same spiritual reason. So while Dion Fortune was distancing herself from all would-be Messiahs, and busily creating all those things on the outer plane that were necessary for her Fraternity to function as an outer court to the Golden Dawn, Crowley found himself at a crucial stage in his life being invited to assume the mantle of the International Head of the Ordo Templi Orientis.

The Abbey of Thelema had died a death. The Argenteum Astrum muttered, stuttered, and generally groaned along after a promising start, but the O. T. O. provided Crowley with a platform which ensured that the Logos is still being heard today, generations after the Beast's death.

⁓

This happened because a certain Heinrich Tränker from Thüringen in Germany, who was known in occult circles as Frater Recnartus, had had a vision in which he saw Crowley as the leader of a group of Masters. Germany was far more receptive to the Master Therion's writings and the *Book of the Law* than his fellow Englishmen—which is probably why he felt that *Liber al vel Legis* was a suitable book to send to Hitler.

Herr Tränker was at that time the leader of a group known as Pansophia, but when a power vacuum occurred within the O. T. O. in Germany following the death of Theodore Reuss, he found himself heading the German branches. As the International Headship of the O. T. O. was now vacant, Tränker's vision was crystal clear: Crowley was to become the supreme head of the whole organisation. The Germans probably knew far less about his notoriety in the British and

American popular press, but in any case were naturally far more receptive to his ideas on Sexual Magick.

The O. T. O., like the Golden Dawn, was originally based upon Freemasonry. Its membership is based upon a system of spiritual training and progressive initiation aimed at helping each person achieve gnosis—personal knowledge of the Gods. As Crowley wrote in his *Confessions*:

> [T]he O. T. O. is in possession of one supreme secret. The whole of its system [is] directed towards communicating to its members, by progressively plain hints, this all-important instruction . . . I accordingly constructed a series of rituals, Minerval, Man, Magician, Master-Magician, Perfect Magician and Perfect Initiate, which should illustrate the course of human life in its largest philosophical aspect.

In his restructured Higher Degrees, VIII–XI, the initiates would learn masturbatory or autosexual magical techniques, heterosexual magical techniques, and techniques utilising anal intercourse. Well, he never said illumination was going to be easy.

Although he was already head of the O. T. O. within Great Britain, this promotion to the supreme pinnacle of the Order worldwide was the saving of Sir Crowley, as some of them charmingly called him. Despite opposition from some existing members, and the obligatory magickal attacks (during one of which the Beast was seen as being protected by an inverted cone of blue light), he remained as Head of the O. T. O. for the rest of his life. With the arrival on the scene of Karl Germer, who accepted Crowley the Mage and the direction in which he would take the O. T. O., the Englishman at last had modest but fairly regular funds and the degree of support he sorely needed. Now that he had achieved that impossibly difficult grade of Ipsissimus, while in Paris, it was the least he could expect.

The whole issue of becoming an 'Adept' has been so muddied by human egos (and the Adepts within the Golden Dawn were the worst culprits of all) that it might be wise to pause and look at what this really means.

Within all the magical and magickal groups there was—and still is—a progressive series of initiations. Even within something as free-spirited as modern Wicca there are generally three degrees. Free-masons have anything up to thirty-three, while magicians using the Golden Dawn system, based upon the kabbalistic Tree of Life, had ten. Both Crowley and Fortune were familiar with these, though the FIL did not use them. In simple terms, the grades of initiation within the Golden Dawn, starting with the most mundane, were:

First Order

Introduction—Neophyte 0-0

Zelator	1–10		Malkuth
Theoricus	2–9		Yesod
Practicus	3–8		Hod
Philosophus		4–7	Netzach

Second Order

Intermediate—Portal Grade

Adeptus Minor	5–6	Tiphereth
Adeptus Major	6–5	Geburah
Adeptus Exemptus	7–4	Chesed

Third Order

Magister Templi	8–3	Binah
Magus	9–2	Chockmah
Ipsissimus	10–1	Kether

The paired numbers attached to the Grades relate to positions on the Tree of Life. The Neophyte Grade of 0–0 indicates that the candidate has not even set foot upon the Tree. For the others, the first number is the number of steps up from Malkuth at the very bottom, and the second number is the number of steps down from Kether at the sublime summit.

What invariably happens, if the teacher in charge is not strict, is that everyone naturally tends to make a frantic dash to get the title of Adept, whether they merit it or not. The fact is, ritual initiations on their own do absolutely nothing to enhance a person's inner stature. The true meaning of being an Adept or High Priest/ess is that the individual has, through hard and lengthy effort, made conscious inner contacts with what might be thought of as Higher Beings, and is now in a position to teach others, and above all accept full responsibility for all the things that might happen when doorways into other realms are opened.

Grades should be descriptions of function rather than status. Thus, an initiate of Tiphereth (and therefore a Priest of the Sun) is in no way superior to someone who has entered the grade of Yesod, and become a Priestess of the Moon.

Though DF never claimed anything grandiose for herself, other than admitting she was an initiate, she seems to have received the 5–6 degree with her husband at the Hermes Temple. By any definition, however, Dion Fortune in the mid-1920s was an Adept in the true sense of the word, and this was reflected by the formation of the group which she governed—with the modest title of Warden—right wisely for the duration of her life.

Aleister Crowley, on the other hand, by his own proclamation, achieved the Ipsissimus Grade in Paris after what he termed the 'Supreme Ordeal', taking himself to a level beyond the Gods and their rules, later commenting: 'I have mastered every mode of my mind, and made myself a morality more severe than any other in the world if only by virtue of its absolute freedom from any code of conduct'.[13]

Unfortunately, because so many people have claimed the same grade before and since (some of them clearly insane), no one can really say how accurate Crowley's self-assessment was. But it is certainly a fact that Crowley the Man's refusal to accept any responsibility for his actions did a lot of people close to him enormous damage, on every level, and it's perhaps only later generations who have achieved various kinds of personal freedom and gnosis because of his Magick.

When it came to her Fraternity, Dion seems to have gone out of her way to avoid the kind of ego ascensions that the Golden Dawn's grade structure tended to inspire. After the obligatory study period, if the candidate passed muster, there was:

1. **Initiation:** in which the aspirant becomes a Priest after the Order of Melchizadek.
2. **The Lesser Mysteries:** of which there were three rites or degrees, linked with the Sacred Mountain on lost Atlantis, each rite awakening contact with an Inner Plane Adept, the identities of which was a closely guarded secret for purely technical reasons.
3. **The Greater Mysteries,** which consisted of:
   a) The Outer Greater Mysteries—in which rituals such as the Rite of Pan and the Isis Rite were performed
   b) The Inner Greater Mysteries

It seems that although DF aspired to open the Inner Greater Mysteries within the lodge, she died before she could do so. However,

---

13. John Symonds, *The Great Beast*.

she was so powerfully present there *after* her death, thanks to the mediators Ann Grieg and Margaret Lumley Brown, that she completed the Arthurian Formula during this post-death period that she had begun with Maiya Tranchell Hayes a few years earlier.

⁓

At this time, when the Great Wild Beast was heading toward his apotheosis in Paris, causing havoc all around as Beasts must necessarily do, Dion Fortune was quietly bringing through from her inner-plane contacts—her Masters—what she felt was one of the most important teachings she had ever received. In effect, this Moon Priestess had had a sort of vision of the machinery of the universe, and now had some idea how everything was put together and how it all worked in all the worlds. It was this complex and challenging document, *The Cosmic Doctrine* (which became a confidential study for her seniors, as it was not published publicly until 1949), which she felt represented the quality and status of her organisation.

Understand this: she did not write it, any more than Crowley wrote the *Book of the Law*. *The Cosmic Doctrine* was 'received', as they said then, in 1923–24—in fact after the death of her beloved teacher Dr Moriarty. It is quite possible that he was one of the inner-plane communicators that apparently had to bring it through in relays of consciousness from very great depths indeed. So what is it about?

If you could see into the mind of God—which is also the same as seeing into the manifest and unmanifest Universe—and if you could analyse its structure as scientists today can analyse DNA, then this is something of what the *Cos. Doc.*, as they called it, tried to express. Quite apart from the complex geometries, the text also looks at qualities such as Good and Evil as though they are lubricating liquids within a machine, rather than mere moral qualities within man. The Master communicated:

You are now in a position to know why the mystery of evil is the secret of the initiates, because when you understand evil it is exceedingly useful. But the undisciplined man, if he knew the usefulness and goodness of evil, would use it dynamically on the positive side of its manifestation, not statically by availing himself of its negative qualities as does the Initiate. You see, it is a matter of geometry . . . [14]

The book describes the mysteries of Space and Time and the true nature of the entities which inhabit these parameters, including the Planetary Being in which each of us is embedded, and through which we draw our earth-lives. According to Dion's vision, the Planetary Being is a vast Elemental composed of the consciousness of, well, everything and everyone. Every human, bird, beast, flower, and insect that ever has been or ever will be.

As we will see in a later chapter, this seminal and exceedingly difficult text is very different to Crowley's equivalent but infinitely more accessible opus.

Meanwhile, at an age when many men start looking forward to the bliss and quiet of tending their vegetable gardens, Crowley had left his Abbey behind, discarded his immediate concubines and disciples (leaving them to starve), and discovered yet another Scarlet Woman, Dorothy Olsen, with whom he travelled across Europe promoting himself as *the* World Teacher, then rode across the Eastern Desert of the Sahara on a camel with her. Exhausting and discarding Dorothy, too, he then took up with the woman who would become his second wife: Maria Teresa Ferrari de Miramar, whom he thought of as a High Priestess of Voodoo and gave the pet name of 'Old Nile'.

---

14. Dion Fortune, *The Cosmic Doctrine* (York Beach, ME: Weiser, 2000), p. 25.

The staid *Times* announced his marriage with an almost respectful piece, which shows that not all newspapers had been sold on the idea of him being the Wickedest Man in the World:

> Mr. Edward Alexander (Aleister) Crowley, the English mystic writer, has been married at Leipzig to Mlle. Maria Teresa Ferrari de Miramar, who is a native of Nicaragua. The marriage ceremony, according to an announcement, was performed in the presence of the British Consul . . .

> Mr. Aleister Crowley was recently refused the right to stay in France. He stated that his fiancee had also been forced to leave France.

> Mr. Crowley was born at Leamington fifty-three years ago and was educated in Malvern and Trinity College, Cambridge. He had been through China on foot, has been received by the sacred lamas in Thibet, and has reached other remote places, such as the Yucatan Peninsula in Mexico.

> He came into prominence in London in 1911 when his picture was painted by Augustus John.

> During the war he went to America and participated in German counter-espionage, declaring that he did this at the request of the British Naval Intelligence Department.[15]

That marriage was doomed of course, like all Crowley's relationships. Then again, he had so many of them, in endless succession, some of them only lasting for furtive minutes, many of them for years but invariably one-sided, that any man with a libido has to admire him for his infinite pulling power.

---

15. The *Times* (London), 19 August 1929.

Perhaps love—or something approaching it—was in the aethers then, because in 1927 Dion Fortune took off her mask for a time to be the very human and womanly Violet Firth, married the newly qualified Dr Thomas Penry Evans, and thus became known proudly, as the convention of the time had it, as Mrs Penry Evans.

A Welshman from a working class background who saw active service in the 1914–18 war with the elite Artists' Rifles, Merl (as they all called him) was seen by most as something of a catch. Why, they wondered, would someone as handsome as Penry take up with someone who was never a great beauty, in an era when women grossly outnumbered the survivors of what was known sombrely in Britain as The Great War of 1914–18. It was estimated that something like two million women had to spend the rest of their lives without mates, because the carnage on the battlefields of Flanders had been so great. He could have had his pick—and it was rumoured that he sometimes did. Christine Hartley, who was Dion's heir apparent for a time, told me that he was an enormously attractive and magnetic individual when you were able to talk to him on a one-to-one basis, but that his wife made sure this wasn't allowed to happen too often. He was also, within the lodge, a superb magician.

In her writings Dion gave the impression that actual intercourse was far less effective than the magical to and fro of energies—the *inner* sex—though how much of this took place between Dr and Mrs Evans will never be known. By the time that Crowley was writing about them in his diary, and inviting the pair around for one of his famous chillis, their marriage was already breaking up, and people recall how she started nagging him unmercifully. Although he gained a reputation for being henpecked, the term 'long-suffering' was perhaps more appropriate. If it was difficult for Crowley's women being partnered with the Logos, it can't have been any easier being married to the Shakti of the Age. And apart from that, it was said that Charles

Loveday and Dion had part-funded his medical studies, so that he qualified as a doctor and no doubt felt eternally in their debt.

Poor Penry didn't stand a chance in some ways. There he was, a working-class rough diamond in an era when such things as social background were of prime importance. Although having seen heavy fighting as a young man during the Great War, he emerged from that conflict as a private, and now ten years later found himself in an upperish-class milieu wherein some of the males were Captains, Majors, and Lt Colonels—though none of them had fought in the trenches in Flanders or seen the slaughter he had, and which he had helped inflict, being a machine-gunner in an elite battalion.

Nevertheless, it was Penry, whom they thought of as Merlin, who seems to have brought through the Celtic energies of the lodge, and removed the last possibility of it ever being influenced again by anything as seemingly ridiculous as the Krishnamurti cultus which had occupied so many people's hearts and minds for the previous decade or more. Really, you cannot take into account the phenomenon of 'Dion Fortune' without giving credit to her husband.[16]

In 1927, when her reputation was beginning to spread, she had a visit from the fourteen-year-old William G. Gray:

> I decided to make a call on Dion Fortune whose London address I had obtained from the *Occult Review*. Getting there was an easy matter, but meeting the lady in question was quite another affair altogether. The female dragon on the doorstep was enough to discourage anyone, but after some argument I was admitted and told rather rudely to await the presence in a somewhat chilly sort of library. Mysterious gongs or bells occasionally sounded in other parts of the house, and once someone opened the door peered round it at me and went away again without a word. I thought I

---

16. See *Priestess: The Life and Magic of Dion Fortune* by Alan Richardson (revised and expanded edition only) for further details of this very humane mage.

detected a faint small of incense as the door closed. There were no clocks in the room and I did not then possess a watch, but it seemed to me a long time was passing.

Eventually the door opened briskly, and Dion Fortune entered accompanied by a different type of dragon who simply sat, in a distant corner of the room staring at me silently. 'Well young man', said DF, 'they tell me you are a most persistent person who refuses to go away when requested. I don't have much time today, so tell me as quickly and clearly as you can what you are looking for'. She sat in the chair immediately facing me and waited for my reply which I had rehearsed to myself in advance. I explained that I was dedicated to occultism, greatly desired to learn everything there was to know about it, had heard she was running an organisation which dealt with it, and how could she help me. She immediately asked the single question I had feared. 'How old are you?' Whereupon I had to confess I was just fourteen and expected to leave school very shortly. She then told me briefly that her Society did not accept members under the age of twenty-one, and she certainly could do nothing whatever without my parents' written consent, nor would she indeed ever think of accepting an under-age candidate. In any case there was a longish study period required before anyone was considered for membership. Those were the rules and she had not made them to be broken by herself or anyone else on any account. She was sorry and wished me well, but that was that and when I was older and more experienced I could always apply again. She would await that date with interest and good afternoon to me. So saying she quitted the room quickly, and the hitherto silent woman rose and beckoned to me with the single word 'Come', then led me to the outer door which she closed after me without another sound. Although everything had been absolutely correct, I felt utterly rejected.[17]

(In point of fact, as Bill told me sixty years later, she had been perfectly correct in her response. In the decades later, when Bill came to

---

17. Alan Richardson and Marcus Claridge, *The Old Sod: The Odd Life and Inner Work of William G. Gray* (London: Ignotus Press, 2003).

be one of the most original interpreters of her Magic, she was a very potent contact of his on the inner planes.)

Compare this to the response of Crowley when the young and equally magic-obsessed Israel Regardie met him for the first time, having ignored his advice to relinquish all his interests in magick, to walk and work his way around the world, and familiarise himself with every conceivable vice. The Master Therion said: "'Got any money on you, Regardie?' and like the young fool I was, I handed it over [\$1200] and he went and spent it on champagne and brandy— always the best for him—and I never saw it again'.[18]

However, to be fair to 'the old man', as Regardie called him, he did make it up to him later in other ways, so that he felt justice had been done.

⁓

Looking at both AC and DF from this distance, it is apparent that they were both obsessed by the 'Sex Question' as it was called then— or more usually the 'Sex Problem'.

To the Great Beast, however, there was neither question nor problem: he rutted like no Mage has done before or since, and constantly did what he wilt.

Whereas Violet . . . she wrestled and fought, inwardly and outwardly, and probably never did win through to gnosis in this area, despite publishing *The Esoteric Philosophy of Love and Marriage*, which seems unbelievably tame today, but was startling enough in 1922 to almost get her expelled from The Golden Dawn for revealing its secrets. In her two books written as Violet Firth, *Machinery of the Mind* (1922) and *The Problem of Purity* (1927), she spends a great amount of time analysing what seemed to be the most pressing issue of the time.

---

18. Quoted in Sutin, *Do What Thou Wilt*, p. 337.

In the chapter entitled 'Sublimation' in the former book, she wrote of sex:

> This great instinct, in its mental and physical aspects, is so fundamental and so powerful that it cannot, with safety to the individual, be entirely repressed, nor, with safety to society be given free rein. We are on the horns of a dilemma, for social laws demand that it shall only be expressed under very limited conditions, those of legal marriage and even then not to an unlimited extent; and nature demands that it shall be expressed as soon as the physical organs of its manifestation are sufficiently developed to function.

This was before she had ever met Crowley, and was written at the time when he was in Cefalu going out of his way never to repress or sublimate the merest surge of his own sexual impulses. She then goes on to show something of the society she lived in by adding:

> The average man solves this problem for himself by conniving at the maintenance of a pariah class of women whose very existence is socially ignored and is a fertile source of misery, disease, and crime. But for women, unless they are prepared permanently to join the pariah class, a social safety valve does not exist and we find among them a much higher percentage than among men, suffering from those nervous troubles that are due to a repression of the sex instinct. This also applies to men who, whether from idealism or fear of disease, do not avail themselves of a compromise.

One does not need the insight of an Ipsissimus to guess what the Master Therion might have said if he had read this. To her, the whole fabric of civilisation was threatened by this problem of sexual frustration and guilt, but she was at least heartened that modern psychology had at last found a solution:

> This problem would prove as intractable in the future as it has in the past were it not that we now know that the law of transmuta-

tion of energy from one form to another is as true for psychology as it is for physics. The conversion is technically known as SUBLIMATION.

But how, in actual practice, could this be achieved? She gives us the answer:

> First, by altering our entire attitude toward sex and realising that a problem is not solved by ignoring its existence. Secondly, by taking the sex problem out of the domain of the subconscious into the conscious mind and frankly facing it, and acquiring dominion over it by the practice of thought control, transmuting our emotions instead of repressing them. Thirdly, by providing a channel of creative interest down which may flow the energies we wish to deflect from their primitive channel of manifestation.[19]

She can't have been too successful at sublimating her own seething desires, because five years later she was writing *The Problem of Purity*, a title with which the Beast would have heartily agreed: purity was a problem. If you were that way inclined, that is, and had never heard of the Law of Thelema, or understood its liberating subtleties.

In this book she inadvertently suggested some techniques that would not have been out of place in the IX° of the O. T. O., suggesting a method of, in effect, 'magical masturbation' aimed at relieving the worst of the tensions engendered by celibacy.

'Next', she wrote, 'visualise the spine as a hollow tube and make a mental picture of your hand encircling it, and then, with this imaginary hand, begin to massage the spine with an upward, squeezing action. Supposing you had a length of soft rubber tubing that had become blocked by some sediment, you could get rid of the obstruction and empty the tube by drawing it through your fist, squeezing it as it went, and so pushing the substance it contained on ahead of the

---

19. For what it is worth, as I typed up these words I clearly heard Crowley in my head saying: 'Sublimation my arse . . .'

constriction in the tube made by the pressure of your fingers. It is the same process that you are to use in imagination on the spine . . . by repeated pushes, gradually working your way up the spine with a stroking action . . . '

From there, as the energies entered the brain, they were to be directed to the intellectual centres in the forehead, where the celibate was then to visualise the ajna chakra, or the Third Eye. Then, she had to imagine herself looking out on to the world from a great height; and project the energy that had been dragged up from the basal chakra out in a radiant stream toward some charitable organisation, willing this energy to be a driving force behind the movement. She suggested, with no sense of irony, the Save the Children Fund.

It's easy to laugh at that now, but if we have a certain level of sexual awareness and security here in the twenty-first century, it is due in no small part to Crowley breaking down all the taboos generations before us, and emboldening others to take his lead in the best of ways.[20]

Yet if both AC and DF had spent their whole lives wrestling with or indulging in the 'Sex Question', neither of them ever quite managed to find real fulfilment with that infinitely more challenging and profoundly more important initiation, the Love Question . . .

---

20. As late as the 1950s, dictionaries in Britain defined the word *masturbation* (when they dared mention it at all) as 'bodily self-pollution', or as 'self-abuse'.

chapter five

INITIATIONS AND OTHER AWAKENINGS

In 1910, at the same time as Crowley's first wife and first Scarlet Woman, Rose, was being committed to a lunatic asylum on evidence supplied by her husband, young Violet Firth was having her first and certainly her last nervous breakdown as a direct result of occult forces she had not yet begun to understand. This happened near the small town of Studley, in the county of Warwickshire, only a dozen miles from where Crowley was born and grew up.

Studley College, where she was a twenty-year-old senior student, was essentially an agriculture college, although there was a hidden agenda behind its curriculum as we will see in the next chapter. The nervous breakdown was caused by the Warden of the college who, Dion wrote, ' . . . had a considerable knowledge of occultism obtained during a long residence in India, and concerning which she used to drop hints that I could make nothing of at the time, but which, in the light of later knowledge, I have come to understand'.[1]

Although she seems to have been quite happy as a student for much of the time, she came to believe that the Warden was using mind-power techniques to control certain individuals and rob them of their money.

---

1. Dion Fortune, *Psychic Self-Defence*, p. xvii.

The woman in question was Dr Lilias Hamilton (c. 1857–1925), who had qualified as an MD at the University of Edinburgh at a time when it was highly unusual to find females in that profession. Later she became head of the Women's Hospital in Calcutta and was then approached by the Emir of Afghanistan to become his personal physician. In her unpublished novel, ominously entitled *The Power That Walks in Darkness*, she told of her time there, her mere presence risking the wrath of the Emir's many wives. Dr Hamilton, who was a real doctor unlike Dr Moriarty, rode motorcycles, slept out on the lawn under the stars, wore clothes that were outrageous for the times, and was a charismatic, often frightening, always inspiring Woman of Power decades before the term was coined. If her story was ever told in full it would probably be every bit as unusual as that of her pupil. Whether she really did have and use occult powers, or whether Violet was manifesting the paranoia attendant upon her psychological problems, is a moot point. Certainly, other students saw nothing sinister in their Warden at all.[2] Yet as she tells it in *Psychic Self-Defence*, if she had not kept a diary recording the actual events of the days, Dr Hamilton's hypnotic suggestions might have robbed her of all sense of reality.

It came to a climax when young Violet, suspecting that one of the less able residents with what we would now call learning disabilities was being mentally manipulated also, managed to rescue the lady in question, and send her off to a safe place with relatives. When the furious Warden found out, Violet was summoned to her office, was fixed with an intent gaze, and without the older woman arguing or abusing, inflicted a litany that was calculated to remove any remains of confidence that Violet had ever had: 'You are incompetent, and you know it. You have no self-confidence, and you have got to admit it', said the Warden, keeping this up for four hours, during which Violet knew that her very soul was in danger and felt walls of darkness

2. Janine Chapman gives a brilliant analysis of Violet's time at Studley in her book *The Quest for Dion Fortune* (York Beach, ME: Weiser, 1993).

encroaching. Finally, having the sense to say all the right things and promise to be a good little Violet from then on, her employer let her go. 'I entered [that room] a strong and healthy girl. I left it a mental and physical wreck and was ill for three years'.[3]

The events are told in some detail, but tend to create more mystification than clarity. Anyone with any magical experience can confirm that when the etheric aura (for this is such a thing) gets damaged and leaks prana, that the symptoms are exactly as described by Dion in *Psychic Self-Defence*. And anyone with any real-life experience—occult or otherwise—will know that people exist who really can destroy confidence and reduce their victims to mere shells. In fact, most of us have had employers or even partners like that at some time.

It may well be that Dr Lilias Hamilton really was, herself, a 'Power that walked in Darkness'; she was no doubt an extraordinary and formidable personality. But it is just possible that she was merely the excuse, the rationale if you like, for the breakdown that had been brewing for some time, and that Violet projected everything onto one demonised figure in the shape of the Warden.

What might have caused such a mental state? As we will see in the next chapter, there is a possible clue in the true nature of the College itself, but Dion herself may well have given some hint in *Psychic Self-Defence* again when she wrote:

> Another new friend became interested in my case and hauled me off to the family doctor who bluntly gave it as his opinion that I had been hypnotised. It was before the days of psycho-therapy, and his ministrations to a mind diseased were limited to patting me on the back and giving me a tonic and bromide. The tonic was useful, but the bromide was not, as it lowered my powers of resistance, and I speedily discarded it, preferring to put up with my discomfort rather than to render myself defenceless. For all the time I was obsessed by the fear that this strange force, which had been applied to

---

3. *Psychic Self-Defence*, p. xx.

me so eventually, would be applied again. But although I feared this mysterious power which I now realised was abroad in the world, I cannot tell what a relief it was to me to find that the whole transaction was not an hallucination, but an actual fact that one could rise up and cope with.[4]

It has been said that all hypnosis is self-hypnosis, but we cannot discount the many tales of the Great Beast using his own very formidable talents upon hapless wretches who succumbed to his psychic onslaughts. However, the fact that the doctor Dion saw afterward prescribed her with bromide may be significant. At that time bromide was widely prescribed for epilepsy, and it was thought that epilepsy was caused by masturbation. Bromide, in effect, calmed sexual excitement and so was held to reduce seizures. Even into the 1970s schoolboys were still joking about bromide as a drug that would stop erections. In 1910, being offered bromide was a quite specific statement.

I am not saying that Dion Fortune was an epileptic, although if her great ability as a trance medium was evident even then, it may well have been mistaken for such by her worried parents. But I do think she might have had a disastrous love experience which may have thrown her whole inner stability into question. We cannot mock her for that. Even today, during the present anything-goes era, with massive support systems of every kind available, a love affair gone wrong can cripple the hardiest of souls. Then, in her level of society when there were certain things you just did not talk about, nor even try to understand, it would have been more devastating than we in the twenty-first century can easily understand. This catalytic confrontation with Dr Hamilton and the subsequent breakdown, more than any ceremony in any magical lodge, was one of the true initiations of her life.

4. Ibid., p. xxiii.

This was a crucial year of madness and breakdown for Aleister Crowley, too. Apart from being subjected to magical attacks by his former superior MacGregor Mathers, much of the tension in his life revolved around his wife, Rose. Being a mother to their surviving child, Lola Zaza, as well as a wife to the completely promiscuous Logos of the Aeon had all proved too much. She did what many have done before and since, and took to drink. He had her committed to an asylum.[5]

If the first and probably most important Scarlet Woman had failed, and if the many brief amours (male and female) he had indulged in during his marriage came to naught, 1910 saw the appearance of a young New Zealand woman who would half-heartedly take on the mantle of Scarlet Woman, though never that of legal wife.

Every century has its romantic couples, whose amours have the power to fascinate because of the intensity, sacrifice, or sheer destructiveness, with their grand moments frequently shot through with rare and uncanny beauty. Everyone has their own exemplars in this respect, and they can range from old Merlin and the crafty young enchantress Vivienne, Lancelot and his 'queen beyond compare' Guinevere, or the tragic Abelard and devoted Heloise, through to modern icons such as Scott and Zelda Fitzgerald, Caitlin and Dylan Thomas, D. H. Lawrence and Frieda, Laurence Olivier and Vivien Leigh, up to and infinitely beyond the nastily self-destructive pairing of Sid Vicious and Nancy Spungen. There was always deep love—as best as each one understood it—plus great, usually unavoidable pain. Most people never get one such relationship in their lifetime, and if they do, and if they survive it, their souls are marked forever.

Aleister Crowley, you have to understand, had an endless succession of such, with his near-endless Scarlet Women, each one neatly noted in his extensive Magical Record. If, during his drug-riddled time on Cefalu with poor Leah Hirsig, the pair of them were closer to

---

5. She seems to have made a full recovery, and later remarried.

Sid and Nancy, then over ten years earlier he had been a bit closer to the Merlin/Vivienne archetype with the enchanting Leila Waddell.

Laylah, as he called her, was the daughter of Irish immigrants to Australia. She moved extensively in the arts scene and was a talented musician, being the lead violin in a women's orchestra. Besotted with her as he was, initially, with all his women, he immortalised her in *The Book of Lies* and his *Confessions*, but she never wanted to give the unreserved dedication to Magick that Leah Hirsig, her main successor, gave. What attracted Laylah to Crowley?

Well, this period was in many ways something of a high-water mark for him. Physically he was still an impressive young man with something leonine about him and a very deserved reputation as a bold adventurer. His erstwhile brother-in-law Gerald Kelly described him as an extrovert type: sunny, humorous, athletic, good at everything, good looking. He was well read, wrote verses 'which he didn't pretend were poetry', and was a very rich man. Though Sir Gerald added, dating himself and his own world: 'the only thing was—he was not a *gentleman*'. Not being a *gentleman* was not something that would have worried an Australian like Leila Waddell. Life with the Beast at this period would have been *so* exciting.

Before he attracted the venom of the popular press, the publicity he had received was, on the whole, more intrigued than hostile. When, in 1910, his former superior MacGregor Mathers had taken him to court for publishing secrets of the GD in his new bi-annual publication, *The Equinox*, the affair became known as the Rosicrucian Rites trial, with all the glamour but essential respectability that the term *Rosicrucian* evokes. As a result, various occult groups and self-styled Orders across the globe had offered him grand and honorary titles.

However, when he decided later in that year to give public performances of the Rites of Eleusis, the Master Therion's little group were not now seen as mysterious Rosicrucians but as 'a blasphemous sect whose proceedings conceivably lend themselves to immorality of the most revolting character', as wrote the journalist from the *Looking Glass*, going on to ask whether it was ' . . . fitting and right that young girls and married women should be allowed to attend such performances under the guise of the cult of a new religion'.[6]

The Rites themselves were a series of public invocations centred on one of the seven planets of antiquity. Far from being revolting, J. F. C. Fuller took his wife and mother to all of them, and observed no impropriety at all, even by the prim standards of the time. Some found them stupefyingly dull. Others were deeply moved. It should be noted that on arrival spectators were offered a brownish drink beforehand which tasted like rotten apples, and contained 'alkaloids of opium'.

The principal members of the troupe were himself, Leila (who played the violin rather than declaimed), and Victor Neuburg, a fellow Cambridge man, who invoked the Gods on stage and summoned up demons in his own soul, and was never able to get Crowley out of his head for as long as he lived.

Young Violet, who still had Dr Hamilton's destructive mantra in her own head, and was trying to track down and put together the broken bits and pieces of her psyche, now did what so many people do who have suffered in this way: she took up the study of psychology. Psychology, she felt, would put all things on a rational basis.

Psychoanalysis and all its related aspects is such an all-pervasive aspect of modern twenty-first century society that we can almost accept it without question as something mainstream, having passed all the rigid tests and scrutinies of Dame Science. In 1910, however, when Violet Firth was recovering from her breakdown, the staid British Medical Association was still undecided about its merits. It

6. *The Looking Glass*, 29 October 1910.

smacked to many of them as something of a fad, and was seen in the same light as the present populist and celebrity passions for Scientology and Kabbalah.

The main gurus of this new movement were of course Freud, Jung, and Adler.

Adler, with his assertions that all humans strive toward power.

Freud, with his emphasis on the 'love experience'.

Jung, with his ideas on the archetypes and the inward alchemies.

In fact, a crucial part of DF's later teachings involved the three rays of Power, Love, and Wisdom that these men exemplified, and in fact in her later life she visited a Jungian analyst for help with her own inner problems—whatever they were. Perhaps by that time she had seen through her own sexual torments and seen through Freud too, for the good doctor had always suppressed certain aspects of his casework which would have pulled his whole thesis to the ground had they been admitted at the time.[7]

It is known that DF communicated with Jung himself, though no trace of their correspondences has survived. Jung, in fact, was a magician pure and simple who secretly believed he was the avatar of the Gnostic god Aion, and who used his powerful and persuasive language to give his purely mystical work an academic veneer, only taking on clients whose visions were in accord with his own notions, and who could afford him. Crowley saw through him when he wrote that in Jung's work 'we see Science gracefully bowing her maiden brows before her old father, Magic'.[8]

One of the great attractions for those who sought to practise psychology was the fact that it was unregulated. Anyone could practise. No qualifications were needed. It was the alternative therapy of the

---

7. In this respect, see Richard Noll, *The Aryan Christ: The Secret Life of Carl Jung* (New York: Random House, 1997) and Jeffrey Moussaieff Masson, *Final Analysis: The Making and Unmaking of a Psychoanalyst* (New York: Ballantine, 2003).

8. Quoted in Deirdre Bair, *Jung: A Biography* (Boston: Little, Brown and Co., 2003), p. 306.

time. And until the staid but all-powerful British Medical Association brought in a requirement for properly qualified practitioners,
Miss Violet Firth became for a time—at the age of twenty-three—
the highest-paid lay analyst in London, working under the aegis of
The Society for the Study of Orthopsychics, in Brunswick Square.

As to her clients, well, by her own admission these included what
she termed as abnormal deviants of both the male and female sex—
that is to say, homosexuals; there were a number of unmarried mothers;
mostly her waiting room was filled with compulsive masturbators.

It is easy to laugh now, but it's an indication of how much of a
problem 'Sex' was in that era, and why the tricky issue of masturbation was dealt with in what must have been a staggeringly forthright
way in Violet Firth's writings.

That 'Sex' was a problem, and caused such inner torment, was entirely because of the overwhelming power of that sterility cult known
as Christianity. What the world needed at that time, were some role
models/idol breakers who could show that sex and religion, orgasm
and god-consciousness were not contradictory and mutually exclu-
sive. And in the figures of DF and AC, that is exactly what the world
was getting just then: it would just take them both a little while to
sort things out for themselves . . .

Crowley, of course, who later described himself (and truly believed it) as a Master Psychologist, was having no trouble in finding
what to do with his own excess sexual and psychic energies—and
bromides played no part in it. Instead, he had the lovely and classy
Leila Waddell and the ever-compliant Victor Neuburg to help him
with his inevitable ascent to god-head. Ironically, it was the latter
who was to prove crucial in bringing through the revelations of the
Aeon.

As a boy William G. Gray had firsthand experience of both Crowley and Neubeurg, and remembered the latter as one of the gentlest men he had ever met. Gray's mother was great friends with his female companion and protector, whom she called Saga. During those visits he heard how Crowley could hypnotise Victor with ridiculous ease and especially liked to do so before company in order to impress them with his evident 'powers':

> He would make Newberg [*sic*] behave like a dog barking and grovelling at his master's feet. Then he would order poor Victor to empty his pockets of money and hand it over immediately. Since his father was usually generous there might be as much as five pounds on his person. Crowley would throw back about half a crown contemptuously saying: 'Get yourself some fish and chips. We're going to the Savoy with the rest', and forthwith do so. In those days it was perfectly possible, and there could even be change left over.[9]

As Jean Overton Fuller found out when researching 'Vicky', as they called him, several people who had known him well felt that Victor B. Neuburg was a being belonging to the kingdom of faery which had, by mistake, taken human birth. Nevertheless, although the Great Beast did enormous damage to his disciple in so many ways, Neuburg was not entirely a victim. When Crowley parted with Laylah he took Neuburg with him to the African desert near Bou Saada where Crowley had brought in his rucksack the *Calls for the Thirty Aethyrs*, the angelic communications which had been dictated to John Dee, Elizabeth I's astrologer and resident magus, by Edward Kelly.

At the summit of a small mountain, where they called the fourteenth Aethyr and performed an act of buggery with Victor taking the active role, Crowley had one of his crucial revelations. He had always

---

9. Alan Richardson and Marcus Claridge, *The Old Sod: The Odd Life and Inner Work of William G. Gray*, p. 56.

known that the sexual act did not detract from the glory of God, but it was only in this moment that he realised it could actually be done to the glory of God and made a sacrament. In his own eyes, having resolved all sorts of dualities and oppositions within himself, he was now a Master of the Temple, or 8-3 as it would be notated, and he came down from the mountain with Victor in triumph.

When Neuburg intimated something of this to the young and virginal Jean Fuller, some twenty-five years later, he said with some pride: 'At any rate we did something which has never been done before! Well, not for hundreds of years anyway. We had no predecessors in the times in which we live . . . It's doubtful whether even Dee himself ever called them . . . *We* called them. We went out into the desert and called them'.[10] At that time, looking back with something of the wisdom of hindsight, he also noted with apparent allusion either to himself or more likely his former Master: 'Divine possession is no guarantee of ordinary intelligence'.[11]

When they broke up—or rather when Neuburg managed to detach himself—Crowley ritually cursed his former disciple by bell, book, and candle, as they say, and the younger man commented: 'I had a nervous breakdown. I was completely dazed. I went down into the country . . .', which matches exactly what young Violet Firth had experienced some years earlier.

If Aleister Crowley by this time had become a Master of the Temple, young Violet Firth was making her first contact with Masters of her own. Unlike the average soul in the Theosophical Society, of which she was a member, she did not for one moment believe in the physical existence of the sort of Masters described by Madame Blavatsky and

---

10 Jean Overton Fuller, *The Magical Dilemma of Victor Neuburg* (London: W. H. Allen, 1965), p. 76.

11. Ibid., p. 63.

her followers. On the other hand, she had no doubt whatsoever about their reality on the inner planes.

> I am also of the opinion, in the light of my own experience in the same field, that the tales of personal meetings with the Masters on the physical plane, and all the evidence for their local habitations and names, is also bunkum, and I do not believe that whoever originated these stories, or whoever substantiated them, has ever been sincere.[12]

In fact her own perception of them was rather more subtle than could easily be explained. In an early version of *The Cosmic Doctrine*, one of her own Masters made the comment:

> The Masters as you picture them are all 'imagination'. Note well that I did not say the Masters were imagination: I said 'The Masters as you picture them . . . ' What we are you cannot realise and it is a waste of time to try to do so, but you can imagine us on the astral plane and we can contact you through your imagination, and although your mental picture is not real or actual, the results of it are real and actual.

Nowadays magicians might tend to regard each 'Master' as a kind of node in the Collective Consciousness—multidimensional, multi-faceted, and multi-consciousness—using an historical identity, perhaps, as a way of enabling the all-too-human individual to, in a sense, get a grip.

The first two Masters she met came during a powerful visionary experience. '. . . I knew that one was the Master Jesus; the other I did not know, save that I felt Him to be a tremendous intellectual force. I have since learnt to know Him as the Most Wise, one of the Lords of Mind, on the Hermetic Ray; to the Master Jesus was given the title

12. *The O. E. Library Critic*, April 1937.

of Most Holy, Lord of Compassion'.[13] The former was later revealed
to be a certain Master R. The leading Theosophists, using language
that was ostentatiously trying to conceal, called him 'The Master the
Count'. The Count in this instance was Le Comte de St Germain, a
legendary figure who strode through the centuries, ageless and marvellous, exerting influence upon the courts of kings. The Master R
was one and the same, a later manifestation. His earthly name was
Rakoczi, and he was the leader of a noble and very real Hungarian
family.[14]

The experience was overwhelming. It did not, like Crowley, make
her a Master of the Temple, but it turned Violet Firth ever more surely
toward becoming Dion Fortune.

> During the next three days the memory of my past incarnations
> returned to me, right back to my first initiation in Atlantis; it was a
> practically unbroken record of temple work, save my last incarna-
> tion, which was most lurid, and into which I seemed to pack all the
> experiences I had forgone during the rest of my evolution. Now
> it is quite a simple matter for any one to equip themselves with a
> series of egotistical phantasies by way of past lives, but in my case
> I got back not only the memory of initiations and temple lives, but
> also the memory of the teaching I had received during those lives.
> The Ancient Wisdom is a very intricate and elaborate philosophy
> and science, and I defy anyone to think it out for themselves in
> the course of a few days without any previous study on the sub-
> ject. Therefore I regard the fact that I have never had to work for
> my knowledge of occultism, but have recovered it, not even piece-
> meal, but in the mass from memory, as strong evidence in favour
> of reincarnation.[15]

---

13. *The Cosmic Doctrine.*
14. Alan Richardson, *Priestess: The Life and Magic of Dion Fortune.*
15. Ibid.

Jesus and Rakoczi were Dion's first Masters, but they were not the most important. She was quite candid as to the identities of the former but very secretive about the identities of the three entities that she would meet upon Glastonbury Tor some ten years later, these being: Socrates, Lord Erskine, and David Carstairs. These were her Secret Chiefs. These were the ones who gave her Knowledge. These were the beings who gave her physical temples their energy from the inner planes, and with whom her co-workers ('followers' would be a term she disliked) made—and still make—contacts of their own.

If this was a crucial and true initiation for Violet Firth, one entirely without ritual or ceremony, then Crowley too stumbled into a kind of new beginning with the arrival in his life of Theodore Reuss.

Reuss was Anglo-German, a utopian, journalist, member of the German Secret Service, music-hall singer, champion of Women's Liberation, and keen practitioner of tantric systems. After the death of Carl Kellner, he became head of the O. T. O. As Crowley tells it, the man came to his chambers in Victoria Street and immediately accused the Englishman of betraying the innermost secret of the O. T. O., relating to the IX°. Crowley had no idea what he was talking about, but then Reuss went straight to the bookshelf and took out the *Book of Lies*, opening it to the page which begins: 'Let the Adept be armed with his Magick Rood and provided with his Mystic Rose'. He saw at once what Reuss meant, and the impact of that revelation was enormous: 'It instantly flashed upon me. The entire symbolism not only of free masonry but of many other traditions, blazed upon my spiritual vision. From that moment the O. T. O. assumed its proper importance in my mind. I understood that I held in my hands the key to the future progress of humanity'.[16]

---

16. *Confessions of Aleister Crowley.*

Although Crowley was already an honorary VII° of O. T. O. (based on his previously held 33° in the Scottish Rite), Reuss now made him Grand Master General X° for the O. T. O. in the United Kingdom of Great Britain and Ireland, which was called the Mysteria Mystica Maxima.

As head of this neo-Templar organisation Crowley took on the name Baphomet, and later wrote for Reuss the *Gnostic Mass*. This highly regarded piece was actually written in Russia, which Crowley visited while in charge of a musical troupe known as the Ragged Rag-time Girls, the latter consisting, as he described them, of three dipsomaniacs, four nymphomaniacs, and two hysterical prudes.[17] It is still performed with great and solemn and innocent delight in various places across the world. In return Brother Merlin, as Reuss preferred to be called among his fellow adeptii, waxed lyrical about Thelema, later working hard to translate the *Book of the Law* into German.

The great and much-tested medium Eileen Garrett (1893–1970) met Crowley at this time, and her perceptions are important in that she was able to assess him with more than mortal prejudice. To her, Crowley was 'a rugged athletic man with an undeniable force of personality'.[18] Once, when she was sitting in a café, he came over and took her hand, looked into her eyes, and said: 'You are a pythoness ... and a strong one'. She remembered him looking at her 'intently with half-closed eyes. I remember that his eyes were protruding and his mouth betrayed a sensual nature. He may have been anywhere between thirty-five and forty at the time—but in those days everyone over thirty looked old to me!' He then slipped one of his rings onto her finger, but she took it off and gave it back to him. 'My giggling companions were somewhat surprised, and I, too, was startled not knowing what a pythoness was'.

---

17. I believe that William G. Gray's mother was one of these.
18. All of the Eileen Garrett quotes on this page are from her autobiography, *Many Voices: The Autobiography of a Medium* (New York: Putnam, 1968), p. 59.

She also told how the Great Beast once invited her to attend one of what she termed his Black Masses at his apartment in Fitzroy Square. The room was draped in black, with zodiacal signs embroidered on the draperies, and she noted: '[H]ighly intelligent men and women, both nationally and internationally famous, some of them connected with government, attended these meetings. Some came to partake of a sacred cup in which, it was said, certain aphrodisiac substances were mixed to make union with Aphrodite herself. The girls, "virgins" of the cult, had an eerie glow on their cloaks, and Crowley himself wore a mantle with many zodiacal signs'. There was also a 'small altar with dimmed lights, and the cross was put on the left-hand side. Many of the women wept and made weird sounds such as I have since heard at meetings of the Holy Rollers in North Carolina'. Was this extraordinary woman frightened? No, because as she explained: 'I have really seen more uncanny things in the voodoo rites in Haiti when the gods take control and where there are frequent blood sacrifices. If there was "authority" in Crowley's meetings with Lucifer, I never knew it'.[19]

In July 1914 both Aleister Crowley and Violet Firth found they were being called on by a higher power than any they had yet invoked, and they had to answer it. Unfortunately for them—for the entire Western world—it was not that much-misunderstood and grossly maligned being Lucifer who was to upset everyone's life with a little bit of subtle light-bringing, but that edgy and invariably troublesome spirit known as Wotan, ancient god of storm and frenzy, who was to demand much sacrifice and take millions of lives. And the power that called to them both in this moment of great need was known to them simply as . . . England.

---

19. Eileen Garrett, *Many Voices: The Autobiography of a Medium*, p. 60.

World War I, also known as the First World War, the Great War, and the War to End All Wars, saw more than sixty million European soldiers mobilised between 1914 and 1918. There were over forty million casualties, which included twenty million military and civilian deaths.

Although Carl Jung wrote of Wotan in context of the Second World War, the comments are equally relevant to the Great War, the festering wounds from which laid the basis for the equal frenzy twenty-five years later.: '[H]e is the unleasher of passions and the lust of battle . . . a superlative magician and artist in illusion who is versed in all secrets of an occult nature'.[20]

Actually, that was exactly how Baphomet, the Master Therion, Perdurabo, and the Great Wild Beast saw himself. How did he answer this call?

Well, his years in America from 1914–18 were extraordinarily busy ones. After all, was still a mighty magician devoted to the Great Work.

In 1915 he wrote some excellent pieces on astrology which Evangeline Adams, the celebrity astrologer at that time, published as entirely her own work, without giving Crowley either credit or payment. He also found an erstwhile 'Magical Son' in Charles Stansfield Jones, also known as Frater Achad, who took inspiration from the Master Therion and wrote some excellent books on the Kabbalah (which turned Crowley's correspondences upside down and trumpeted the arrival of the Aeon of Maat) and then went his own way, believing that he had surpassed the older man in terms of status.

By 1916 Crowley had claimed the grade of Magus, and was by now firmly set in his belief and declaration that he, and only he, was the Prophet of the New Aeon—of Horus.

In 1917 he became editor of *The International*, a pro-German magazine; finished *Liber Aleph, the Book of Wisdom or Folly* (which title might well express his own life); and performed the Amalantrah

---

20. Quoted in Paul Bishop, *The Dionysian Self* (Berlin: de Gruyter, 1995), p. 308.

Working with a new Scarlet Woman named Roddie Minor, which seems to have made a rent in the fabric of space and time and brought an extraterrestrial being named 'Lam' into the earth realms. And then he took a Great Magical Retirement on Oesopus Island on New York's Hudson River; published his own version of the *Tao Teh King*; and then during this time met Leah Hirsig, although their relationship would not start immediately.

But during all this there was still the knotty question of the War to End All Wars being waged on the other side of the Atlantic. What did the Great Wild Beast do about this? How did he serve his country?

The fact is at the age of thirty-nine he was too old for active fighting, too disreputable for anything diplomatic, far too unreliable for organising the civilians or bolstering morale. So he did the next most appropriate thing: he became a spy.

⁓

Crowley's Great War was every bit as different and odd as anything else in his odd and different life. To the outsider he spent four years in America deeply involved in anti-British activities, espousing the German and even the Irish causes in ways that marked him as a complete traitor. Typically, that was not the way *he* had seen it.

As he explained in his *Confessions* after the war, not only were his ranting pro-German articles written with such irony, such subtle English tongue-in-cheek absurdity that their effect upon the reader was the opposite of what his Germanic employers had hoped, but that, actually, he had been a double agent all along, and was really in the employ of British Naval Intelligence.

The tendency of even his devoted readers (myself included) has been to raise one cynical eyebrow and write this off as one of Crowley's less pleasant characteristics—an example of him backing the wrong Teutonic and Brythonic horses, then attempting to justify his betrayal with absurd bluster that fooled no one. However, in his excellently researched and frequently jaw-dropping *Secret Agent 666*,

Richard B. Spence demonstrates that the Beast had been telling the truth all along, despite later attempts by members of the Intelligence community to distance themselves from him over the years. Moreover, using documents gleaned from British, American, French, and Italian archives, Spence (who is *not* an occultist nor a Thelemite) shows that Crowley was involved in a plot to overthrow the government of Spain, played a role in thwarting Irish and Indian nationalist conspiracies, and—as we have seen—was linked with the 1941 flight of Rudolf Hess.

But during his time in America the Beast had a specific mission: to gather information and to keep tabs on key members of the German community there, making use of the multiple agent George Viereck (the owner of *The International*), the writer Hanns Heinz Ewers, and carrying up a chain of contacts which included Ambassador Bernstorff. As recounted by a friend of Crowley's, George Langelaan, ' . . . the Germans came to place great faith in the Beast's "intuition" and saw him as an indispensable guide to the mentality of the Americans and the British. He especially impressed them with his ability to predict the actions and reactions of the British. It was almost as though he could see into the inner sanctums of Whitehall'.[21] It never seemed to enter their heads that he was a double agent plying them with false information.

Crowley's role, using careful misinformation and disinformation, was generally to do all he could to bring America into the war on the side of the Allies. And if it meant playing a major role in sinking the RMS Lusitania, then so mote it be . . .

The Lusitania was a British luxury liner that was torpedoed by a German U-boat off the coast of Ireland, killing 1,198 of the people aboard. It was attacked because Crowley had managed to prove to the German authorities that it was carrying large quantities of weapons, and was effectively a man-of-war. The huge loss of innocent civilians

---

21. Ibid., p. 83.

turned public opinion in many countries against Germany, and was a major influence on America's decision to enter the war.

And the Beast was very proud of himself, for what he had achieved.

~

Back in Britain, with growing numbers of men joining the British armed forces during the First World War, and promptly getting slaughtered, the country was desperately short of labour. The government decided that more women would have to become involved in producing food and goods to support the war effort, and so the Women's Land Army was established. It was a sign of those times that some farmers resisted this measure, calling the first volunteers the 'lilac sunbonnet brigade', though it was not so much the femininity they objected to (after all, women had always been busy on farms milking, butter making, poultry keeping, haymaking, and the like) but rather the fact that they would have to deal with 'foreigners'—women from another area, and worst of all another social class. So in 1916 the Board of Trade began sending agricultural organising officers around the country in an effort to persuade farmers to accept these women workers. Eventually, by 1917, there were over 260,000 women working as farm labourers.

The Great Beast had never worked on the land. He had never worked full stop. He had never known what it was like to be a servant to anyone, though he spent many years apeing the gentleman, as his brother-in-law once acutely observed.

From 1916 to 1919 Violet Firth served with the Women's Land Army, using the skills she had been taught in Studley College and also learning something about the 'servant problem' firsthand. As Gareth Knight describes it, her idealism and belief in direct action shone through during the first year she spent on a farm near Bishop's Stortford, on the border between Hertfordshire and Essex. 'When wages were being paid late, tired of evasions and excuses, she stood with the keys of the establishment poised over the sewage tank, and threatened to drop them in unless the money was forthcoming . . . '[22]

After that, a way opened up for her to do work of national importance, and she found herself in charge of a laboratory where research work was being done in connection with foodstuffs. She spent long hours in a large, empty building, watching and waiting while bacterial cultures brewed in an incubator. It was the perfect foundation for everything that followed.

Two things emerged from that time: first, she made the genuinely major discovery of how to manufacture cheese out of vegetable casein—in other words from soya milk. This was the first time anyone had managed to produce a non-animal protein, and she was ahead of her time in this respect alone. She could have made an absolute fortune—no pun intended—had she foreseen the importance of soya in the world to come.

Second, a side effect of the enforced quiet of this work was that her astral sight suddenly opened and gave her—as she described it—one of the great frights of her life. In the darkness, in the silence, with the outside world apparently no longer existing, it would be a surprise if her psychic faculties did *not* open. She had no training at this point, remember. The best she could do was join the Theosophical Society, proposed by Edward L. Gardner—who later became so embroiled with the controversies around the Cottingley Fairies and who little dreamed that his protégée would one day go deeper into the true faery realms than almost anyone before.

Well, she worked away in the darkness, nominally a member of the TS, as everyone called it, and it was while she was afire with this newfound but actually long-buried 'astral sight' that she made her first contact with the Masters. For a while she was taken with the glimpse of the Star in the East as represented by Krishnamurti, but before too long she would quit that night and enter the day because

---

22. Gareth Knight, *Dion Fortune and the Inner Light*, p. 37.

a Golden Dawn would rise in her life and she would never be the same again.

⌒

Violet Firth was initiated into the Alpha et Omega Temple of the Hermetic Order of the Golden Dawn in 1919 and eventually reached the grade of Portal. She took as her Magical Name 'Deo non Fortuna', meaning 'By God and not by Fortune'—hence of course the pen name Dion Fortune. There was no particular meaning behind that choice of name, however. In fact, it was chosen out of snobbery as much as anything. Look at any list of Magical Names from members of the Golden Dawn and you will find established family mottoes, nothing more: Maiya Tranchell Hayes was known as 'Ex Fide Fortis' because it was the traditional family motto of the Beauchamp family, and this was her maiden name; Charles Seymour was 'Foy pour Devoir' because the Seymours of Ireland had always used that as their motto. They invariably used their initials on correspondence, hence: DNF, EFF, FPD, and so on. Interestingly, perhaps because he did not come from an 'old' or top-drawer family like many of the others, Crowley devised his own names (which everyone should), and so his initiation into the same Order was recorded as 'Perdurabo', meaning 'I will endure until the end'. Which is exactly what he did.

Although the AO, as it was called, was under the leadership of the novelist J. W. Brodie-Innes, Dion's immediate teacher seems to have been that influential woman we have already discussed, Maiya Curtis Webb, who later became Maiya Tranchell Hayes. Although she became disillusioned with the first temple, the first feeling was almost one of relief, as if she had come into a harbour after a long storm. This was when the rent in aura caused by Dr Hamilton was finally healed.

Despite this positive effect upon Dion, the AO was just about dead in the water by that time, its glory days gone. In a letter which Maiya wrote to Jane Wolfe, she remembered those times and wrote: 'You talk of my taking charge of the G.D. when B[rodie].I[nnes]. died.

I only wish it had been possible to do so, but there was no one to take charge of, the one or two that I have been in touch with never bothered to keep up with what they knew . . . '[23]

So although the new initiate known as Deo non Fortuna didn't find what she was truly looking for until she joined the Hermes Temple in Bristol, much later, at least the echoes of what had been done within the AO impressed her well enough:

> The effect of the ceremonies and methods taught by MacGregor Mathers was to produce the most remarkable psychic experiences and extensions of consciousness in those who had any psychic capacity at all; the methods and aim of these processes were intelligently taught in the higher grades in certain sections of the order . . . [24]

That was never how Crowley saw it in his own initiation in 1898, however. He wrote:

> I had been most solemnly sworn to inviolable secrecy. The slightest breach of my oath meant that I should incur 'a deadly and hostile current of will, set in motion by the Greatly Honoured Chiefs of the Second order, by the which I should fall slain or paralysed, as if blasted by the lightning flash'. And now I was entrusted with some of these devastating though priceless secrets. They consisted of the Hebrew alphabet, the names of the planets with their attribution to the days of the week, and the ten Sephiroth of the Cabbala. I had known it all for months; and, obviously, any schoolboy in the lower fourth could memorise the whole lecture in twenty-four hours.
>
> I see today that my intellectual snobbery was shallow and stupid. It is vitally necessary to drill the aspirant in the groundwork.

---

23. O. T. O. archives, dated 17 July 1934.
24. 'The Occult Field Today' from Dion Fortune, *Applied Magic*, p. 63.

He must be absolutely familiar with the terminology and theory of Magick from a strictly intellectual standpoint.[25]

In the event, like the sort of errant schoolchildren who eventually prove to be bigger than their schools, they were both expelled from their respective temples. Crowley was booted out because he originally sided with his imperator MacGregor Mathers during an internal schism, and then later fell out with Mathers himself. Dion was expelled by Mrs Mathers because she had, Moina insisted, revealed secrets of the higher teachings in her infinitely inoffensive book *The Esoteric Philosophy of Love and Marriage*. Both of them became subjected to psychic attack as a result: AC from Mr Mathers, DF from Mrs Mathers. Both of them triumphed. Both of them went on to form their own groups and do things their own inner way.

Crowley has been accused of sprinting through the grades after his initiation, mastering them intellectually but perhaps not on deep experiential levels. Then again he never had any peers to tell him to slow down, or point out other approaches. He had fallen out with Mathers, and beyond him there was only Brodie-Innes and Robert Felkin who might have been up to the task of teaching him—but you can bet that he would have fallen out with them, too, had they tried. So what we see is Crowley becoming an Ipsissimus at the level of Kether without ever really learning the very first lesson of Malkuth, which is Discernment.

Yet the Magick was clearly all there within him, and it never left him when things got difficult, and he would have scorned the present-day tendency for people being little more than hobby occultists.

Dion never got too hung up on such things as grades, although toward the end of her life she confessed to her lawyer friend that

---

25. Aleister Crowley, *The Confessions of Aleister Crowley*, p. 170.

she was going through a Geburah initiation—that is to say the trials and torments and tests of the martial energies that constitute the *real* thing, as opposed to the outer ceremonial.

The pair of them, Dion Fortune and Aleister Crowley, were so very obviously born to the magical arts, that eventually you have to ask: How? Where? Why?

chapter six

FALLING TO EARTH
AND OTHER TRAUMA

They were not quite contemporaries.

He had been born on 12 October in 1875.

She was born fifteen years later, on 6 December 1890.

Yet compared to Violet Firth, who had been having visions of what she was certain was lost Atlantis from the time she was four, he was a late starter, not having his first mystical experience until 1896, so they balanced magically if not exactly chronologically. In any case, the fifteen years' difference does not seem to have given him any appreciable advantages in wisdom.

This is where the shaft of the caduceus plunges into the ground, for when the soul falls to earth to be born, as the Gnostics say it does, then its subsequent destiny is defined as much by the energies of the earth beneath, and the accompanying Spirit of Place, as by the stars and planets which seem to be wheeling above. So in the a sense the crucial question is not *when* they were both born, but *where*.

Edward Alexander Crowley—for that was his real name—was born at 30 Clarendon Square, Leamington Spa, in the county of Warwickshire, England. It's a pleasant enough town to visit today, with no public acknowledgement of its notorious son, so it's true enough that a prophet is not without honour save in his own country. Or in this case, his own spa town. Leamington has precious few claims to fame except that it was once regarded as being at the exact middle of England. So in a sense it was the navel, the centre, not just of England but of the British Empire, which, at the time of Crowley's birth, was at its zenith. Where else could Crowley have been born but in the Omphalos of Queen Victoria's planet? Staid little Leamington Spa should have become Thelema's answer to Bethlehem—the centre of the world from which the Logos uttered the Word of the Aeon. Nowadays it boasts about little more than regularly winning the 'Britain in Bloom' competition.

And Violet Mary Firth, this proud and potent Englishwoman, was born in 1890, on 6 December, in Bryn-y-Bia in Llandudno, in the country of the Red Dragon, or Wales.

Any British reader will appreciate the irony of that statement, but it's not easily appreciated by non-Brits what this means.

Wales is not simply a western county of England. No true Welshman would call himself British. Wales is the home of the old Gods, and dragon energies. Yet she never mentioned her birth there, never boasted about it as would any other Welsh-born soul. She did, in one of her novels, mention that the landmass known as the Orme[1] (on which she had been born) was where the Goddess Keridwen minded her cauldron. When her character asked who Keridwen was, he is told that she is: ' . . . the Keltic Ceres, and her cauldron is the prototype of the Graal'.[2]

Although she gave a talk in Llandudno once as Dion Fortune, she never made anything of her Welsh origin. It is said by astrologers that when a person fails to face up to certain aspects within himself or herself, then someone invariably appears who is almost an incar-

---

1. Which means serpent, or dragon.
2. Dion Fortune, *The Winged Bull* (London: SIL, 1999), p. 166.

nation of those qualities. Perhaps that was part of Penry's role, to be the incarnation of the fiercely proud and potent Welsh spirit, and to make her confront that in her psyche which she had always ignored, or avoided.

Many magicians, then and now, have stories to tell about their own births—stories which mark them out as different, or even something akin to a wonderchild. Some of them are actually true. Writing in the third person at the beginning of his *Confessions*, Crowley offered:

> He bore on his body the three most important distinguishing marks of a Buddha. He was tongue-tied, and on the second day of his incarnation a surgeon cut the fraenum linguae. He had also the characteristic membrane, which necessitated an operation for phimosis some three lustres later. Lastly, he had upon the centre of his heart four hairs curling from left to right in the exact form of a Swastika.[3]

Matching that, Patrick Benham, in his book *The Avalonians*, describes how a retired couple came to live next door to Kitty Tudor Pole, who was the sister of the well-known mystic Wellesley Tudor Pole, founder of the Chalice Well Trust in Glastonbury:

> The woman told Kitty a strange tale. Evidently, very soon after the birth of her daughter something had happened to convince her that the child was a changeling: as if something had snatched its soul away to replace it with another. The mother was Sarah Firth; the child was Violet Mary.

---

3. *Confessions of Aleister Crowley*, p. 36.

There had long been a rumour in occult circles that Dion Fortune was the result of an act of fey intervention . . .[4]

$\sim$

Crowley's grandparents were wealthy brewers, and his father and mother were dedicated members of the Plymouth Brethren, which insisted on the literal truth of the Scriptures, a rejection of all priestly authority with all members free to speak as the Holy Spirit moved them, and a belief in the imminence of the Second Coming. In many ways, those principal tenets were also found within Crowleyanity.

Violet Firth's grandparents were hoteliers, involved in the running of various spa hotels that almost had modern-day New Agey–type treatments as standard. They were initially converts to Christian Science, believing that certain aspects of the mind, in tune with the spirit of Christ, could affect real healing among the sick and needy. Later this faded, and her father Arthur became a member of the magical group that she formed, and her mother Sarah was regarded by many as a truly spiritual woman in her own right. Violet never lost her urge to heal, and serve the common folk.

$\sim$

In terms of schooling, and youth, Crowley was seen by himself as the expected Wild Child, and his stories of how he discovered the Three Kings still has the power to amuse.[5] With regard to the most dominant of these 'kings', in respect to his future career, William G. Gray told me something which he got from his mother via Victor Neuburg, and which he felt was crucial to understanding the Old Master, as he liked to call Crowley. I attach this as appendix B.

Violet, as far as anyone knew, was a good little schoolgirl, although Ithell Colquhoun recalled tales of her psychism frightening

---

4. 'Patrick Benham, *The Avalonians* (Glastonbury, UK: Gothic Image Publications, 1993), p. 252.

5. The Smo-King, the Drin-King, and of course the Fuc-King.

her schoolpals. She certainly went to an avant-garde school near Weston-super-Mare, in the west of England, but then when the family
moved to London in 1906 she met one person who would later figure
very prominently in her life: Maiya Tranchell Hayes—or Mrs Curtis
Webb, as she then was.

Bernard Bromage, who was a keen observer of people, clearly fell
under Maiya's spell, too. In his experience the older woman seemed
to know everything there was to be known about occultism, had a
huge and expensive collection of books on all aspects of Magic from
every tradition, and with the help of her faithful servant Thomas
John Manning held benevolent sway over a flat in Kingston House
and also 27a Kensington Square. The rooms of both, he recalled, were
bedecked with witches' rosaries, occult amulets, charms, and numerous potent mandalas.

If there are any mysteries still to be fathomed with regard to Dion
Fortune, they would he held by this woman. Let me make her details
clear for other researchers, because she is the link between the Logos
of the Aeon and the Shakti of the Age . . .

Mabel Gertrude Beauchamp was the eldest daughter of Robert H.
Beauchamp, Esq., of Dublin, and was probably born around 1878. The
motto of the Beauchamp family was 'Ex Fide Fortis'. She married Dr
John Curtis Webb on 30 June 1898, and filed for divorce from same
in 1927, blaming his adultery. By 1934 she was already married to Dr
Edmund Duncan Tranchell Hayes, who was then working at Northampton County Mental Hospital, but that marriage seems to have
foundered, too, as in a letter to Jane Wolfe (one of Crowley's students
from Cefalu) she mentions having taken a large house in Cornwall
with three servants and five large dogs.

After she died in December 1948, nothing was heard of her (on the
outer planes at least) until 1966, when a box containing her magical
impedimenta, which had been buried for years in a cliff-top garden,

was found washed up on a beach between Selsey Bill and Bracklesham Bay in Sussex, after the cliff itself had crumbled. The box contained quarter banners, sceptres, two embroidered stoles, and Egyptian-style headdresses. Francis King wrote about this in his groundbreaking *Ritual Magic in England*, which helped make the ordinary world aware of the secret history of magic. In a strange sense, this appearance of the box washed up on the shore really was a sending from a Sea Priestess to the modern world.

According to Bromage, Maiya had known Dion since she was a girl—presumably they were neighbours in London—and had seen in her from the start 'an individual of strong and talented personality, a poetess of great charm and distinction, and a potential occultist of discernment and cultivation in her chosen province'.[6]

Could she also have met young Violet Firth because of the younger woman's mental health problems? Both her husbands were involved in this field. And she herself had once suffered a nervous breakdown when in the Alpha Omega Temple, which was cured when its alchemist Archibald Cockren gave her just three drops of his carefully prepared oil-of-silver.

∽

These next were Crowley's wonder years. Before the age of thirty-five, before the drugs began to whittle away at his awesome force, he had seen more, done more, than most of us ever will, no matter how long and boldly we live. After matriculating from Trinity College, Cambridge, in 1895 and writing his first pornographic book (*White Stains*), he conducted himself in such a way that he was expelled from individual homes, dining clubs, climbing clubs, brothels, towns, magi-

---

6. Quoted from the article 'Dion Fortune', published in the magazine *Light* in 1960. In her will she left a rare book by John Dee to C. R. Cammell (an early biographer of Crowley), an exotic array of jewellery, and bric-a-brac to many people—largely women—and valuable brooches to her sister Ethel Mary Stoney Archer, from Cheltenham.

cal Orders, and whole countries. He climbed the Matterhorn (with a cow), mastered unconquered peaks in Mexico, and climbed further up Kanchenjunga and K2 than anyone had done before—and without oxygen. He challenged mountains, people, deserts, steppes, Gods and all their morals, and along the way betrayed, inspired, amazed, and disgusted men and women in every part of the world. His sexual appetite was varied, seemingly prodigious, and generally obliged by an endless succession of followers of both sexes. No one ever forgot meeting him.

His initiation into the Hermetic Order of the Golden Dawn took place in 1898. This was when he met the legendary MacGregor Mathers, who with his lovely fey wife Moina was the true genius behind that Order. The poet W. B. Yeats once described Mathers as like a walking flame, and also 'half lunatic, half knave'. Similar might later be said about Crowley, actually, although it would probably be third lunatic, third knave, third genius.

With a large inheritance he bought Boleskine House on the shores of Loch Ness in Scotland where he performed the Abra-Melin Operation in order to find his Holy Guardian Angel, and then proceeded to fall out with just about everyone in the GD, although Mathers initiated him into Adeptship in Paris.

From 1900–04 he travelled and adventured extensively throughout Mexico, Ceylon, India, Burma, and Paris again, where the columnist Wambly Bald saw him years later and wrote:

> At any rate Montparnasse cannot forget this romantic figure who used to stroll to the Dôme or the Coupole in kilties or plus fours, his entire head cleanly shaved save for a single waxed forelock described by himself as 'the Mark of Buddha'. Sometimes he called it his 'Cling-Clong', and he was in the habit of dyeing it pink or saffron to explain his mood.[7]

---

7. Wambly Bald, *On the Left Bank*, edited by Benjamin Franklin V (Athens, OH: Ohio University Press, 1987).

Then he fell out with Mathers, was subjected to magical attacks by same, devised a ritual of Self-Initiation which enabled him to achieve—or so he claimed—the grade of Adeptus Major, devised experiments in Enochian Magic, shot someone, wrote more books on magick and pornography, and married the lovely Rose Kelly, who became his first Scarlet Woman. Besotted, they honeymooned in Paris, Naples, Cairo, and India, and returned to Cairo in April 1904.

And this is when, thanks entirely to Rose, he 'received' the notorious and possibly holy *Book of the Law*. This is when the New Aeon is held to have begun, and every ordinary date since given the suffix by Thelemites as e.v.—*era vulgari*.

But what exactly did he mean when he used the term 'Scarlet Woman'? Martin Booth put it best when he wrote:

> A Scarlet Woman was the term used for a woman who was a medium directly in touch with the gods. She was also, in the form of Lady Babalon, considered the spiritual consort of The Beast 666, upon which she rode. Lady Babalon could reveal herself as a living human, which would be one of her lowest manifestations. In her highest state, she was Shakti, the partner of Shiva in the Hindu pantheon, with whom she was eternally locked in a sexual embrace from the continual orgasm of which came the foundation of the universe and everything in it. She was, in short, mistress of the masters of the universe and, therefore, of the Secret Chiefs.[8]

In personal terms, with respect to Crowley's libido, she also had to have unspeakable or unfathomable desires, which in modern terms might mean she was game for anything.

It was in their Cairo hotel, after demonstrating his powers in the King's Chamber of the Great Pyramid, that the Gods spoke through

---

8. Martin Booth, A *Magick Life* (London: Hodder & Stoughton, 2000), p. 183.

Rose, who revealed herself to be an excellent trance medium. Following her instructions he invoked Horus, and was told that a new Aeon had begun. Then on the 8th, 9th, and 10th of April at exactly noon he heard the voice of Aiwass, his Holy Guardian Angel, dictating the words of what became his sacred text. Aiwass (or Aiwaz) was the minister of Hoor-paar-krat (a version of Horus), the god of force and fire. Crowley caught a glimpse of him and saw him as a tall, dark man in his thirties, with the face of a savage king, but whose eyes were veiled to hide their destructive power.

Although the primary messenger was Aiwass, the *Book of the Law* presented three key personalities to deliver the message, and these are the godforms of the three chapters: Nuit, Hadit, and Ra-Hoor-Khuit.

Parts of the book use the numerical ciphers known as gematria, an aspect of Kabbalah which Dion Fortune later brilliantly described as being like doing mensuration with an elastic ruler, but which Thelemites seem to adore. Aiwass warned that the scribe, Ankh-af-na-khonsu (an Egyptian incarnation of Crowley), was never to attempt to decode the ciphers, for to do so would end only in folly.

The *Book of the Law*, also called *Liber AL*, *Liber Legis*, *Liber AL vel Legis*, or just *AL* is something that everyone must assess themselves, and there are any number of sites online where it can be accessed. To the outsider, it is undeniably beautiful in parts, ostensibly disturbing in others. To the followers of Crowley, it is up there with the sacred texts of Christianity, Buddhism, Islam, and the rest, and they believe earnestly that the world will benefit if only it were adopted.

But what of young and virgin Violet Mary Firth at this time? Did this as-yet-unawakened Priestess of Isis have any sense that aeon-making events were happening to the east, in mystic Egypt? No, not at all. Weston-super-Mare, a small seaside resort, is a far cry from the heat and chaos of Cairo, and it would be some years before Crowley published

Liber AL. But the dozy little town was proving every bit as important to Violet's awakening as Cairo was for Crowley. Not that Miss Firth had glimpsed any sort of savage-faced king like Aiwass, but—unlikely as it may seem—she had clearly connected with an energy that was every bit as potent; she was working with what Robert Graves would later describe as the 'White Goddess': the spirit of the land, seeking voice through poetry. If Crowley was Fire and Air, then she was Earth and Water.

In 1904, while Ankh–f-n-Khonsu was creating the *Book of the Law*, Violet saw the publication of her own book of poetry, aptly called *Violets*, and she followed it up two years later with *More Violets*. The former bore the words in the frontispiece: 'These Poems are offered to the Public in the hope that those to whom the author is now a stranger may some day become her friends'. Which is either the hope of a very lonely child or an extremely secure and affectionate one.

Unlike Crowley's designed-to-shock *White Stains*, there was, not surprisingly for a fourteen-year-old, not a single sexual reference or innuendo, but instead the poems in the two slim volumes were filled with the spirits of the elements, with titles like 'The Hills', 'The Corn Field', 'Music in Nature', and 'The Song of the Sea'. Already the earth and sea Goddesses were beginning to talk to her. In later years they would talk through her. Of them all, the most interesting is perhaps 'The Song of the Sea', written in February 1904, although less because of its content than because of its sense of rhythm. Its opening verses are:

What are the billows murmuring?
Singing so soft and low,
As, retreating, they bare the sea-sands fair
With a ceaseless ebb and flow:

[…]

And fiercely the north wind bellows,
And loudly the billows roar;
With an impotent rage, that nought can assuage,
They rush on the rock-bound shore . . . .

There was also the revealing poem from *More Violets* which she wrote in July 1906, called 'The River of Life':

Where the great grey peaks for ever
Raise their heads towards the sky,
There its fountain has the river,
Flowing onwards, pausing never,
Down to where the willows quiver:
Onwards, downwards, solemn river,
Flowing through eternity.

So my life is ever flowing,
Onwards to the sea,
Down to where the waves are roaring,
And the snow-white gull is soaring—
There at last its waters pouring,
Mingling for eternity.

That, if anything, was a preliminary to her superb prose-poem of *The Sea Priestess*, which stands today as the finest novel on real Magic ever written, a novel that is absolutely soaked with the rhythms of the sea to an almost hypnotic degree, and of which this childhood effort is almost a prophecy.

To what must have been her enormous pride, this first effort was given a handsome review in *The Girls' Realm* in May 1905, with the critic praising young wise young nature-loving Violet and wondering

whether 'Time, the Tester of all things, has indeed in store for us another Elizabeth Barrett Browning, or another Emily Brontë'.

Wise little Violet. Not many people ever used that term in respect
to Crowley, despite the awe they would sometimes feel for his knowledge. Nor could the reviewer have known that one day the young
poet Violet would exist beyond Time, and appear to people in their
dreams, or in vision, directing the currents of their lives. He could
never have imagined the links she would make with a man who was
about to be branded the wickedest in the world.

The year 1905 onward saw more marvels in the life of Aleister
Crowley. After publishing his *Collected Works* (at the age of thirty) he
travelled with Rose across China and started writing his *Liber 777*,
which contains the tables of correspondences which make the Kabbalah work, and which everyone should challenge but so few do. He
achieved the spiritual ecstasy known as Samadhi, but did speculate
as to how much of this was down to the hashish. He no longer had
much interest in searching for or challenging Masters, because in
his own eyes (and those of his followers) he was now a Master in his
own rite/right.

In 1907 he wrote *The Holy Books* and *Konx Om Pax*, and founded
his own Order, the A. A. In this year also he met J. F. C. Fuller, who
totally accepted the Master Therion and all he stood for—until they
fell out. He visited Morocco and then walked across Spain with Victor Neuburg. Then between 1909 and 1913 he published the first ten
volumes of *The Equinox*, at his own expense, never recouping his out-
lay, but never stinting as to quality of production.

And during that time, he also saw the deaths of his children, which
were mentioned in his writings but never seem to have registered
upon him as much as they would on a normal loving father. In fact, he
seemed more keen to blame their mother, Rose. The fact is, even his
most ardent disciples could never have said that he was a good dad.

Crowley fathered several known children by various women, and probably several more as a result of his innumerable brief encounters.[9] In all he had at least five daughters and one son.

Rose had three girls in succession: the splendidly named Isis, Hecate, and Lola Zasa. Only the latter survived to adulthood.

Leah Hirsig gave birth to the baby he called Poupee, and after a long bout of ill health she died in Cefalu.

Deirdre MacAlpine, who confronted him on the steps of the court and demanded to have his child, gave him Aleister Attaturk, in 1937.

And there are persistent claims to being Crowley's son by a man naming himself as Amado Crowley, although virtually nothing is known about the veracity of his claims.

And what of Violet Firth? Apart from joining the Christian Scientists for a time, and having her poem 'Angels' published in their journal, there is little information from that period beyond a rumour—always said with raised eyebrow and dramatic pause—that she went away to the Lake District for a time. The implication here is simply that she was pregnant; and in those days, even among relatively liberal families such as hers seem to have been, this was a great disgrace, an unmentionable mistake. In the lower classes young women who got pregnant outside of holy wedlock were often sent to the workhouse or the local lunatic asylum. Or else the family, if they could afford it, would move to another area, and the new grandmother would bring the child up as her own, the real mother posing as the elder sister.

There is no hard evidence that this ever happened to Violet, except for a Wiccan woman who, in the 1980s, was making discreet claims that she was Violet's illegitimate child, but also more pertinently because of the nature of Studley College. Janine Chapman, who interviewed two very elderly women who had actually been at Studley with Violet

---

9. It is rumoured, for example, that Barbara Bush is his daughter!

pointed out that it was actually a semi-nursing home for neurotic young girls. One of the women in question, Evelyn Heathfield, described her first meeting with Miss Firth:

> She overtook me, and she looked down at me with a sort of smile, and to this *day* I can't remember, but I think she had a tooth missing. It was a crooked smile. She said: 'Oh are you mad? Or don't you get on at home? Or have you been crossed in love?'[10]

It could well be that all three had applied to the nascent Dion Fortune, and that she had been sent there to recover not only from a failed romance, later hinted at in *The Demon Lover*, but the delivery of a child.

---

10. Janine Chapman, *The Quest for Dion Fortune*, p. 165.

seven

PAST LIVES
AND SIMILAR FUTURES

Every magician has memories of what seem to be past lives. No real magician gets too hooked on these, however, and often has very differing notions as to what these may really be. Crowley had a series of these apparent 'far memories' pour through him during his Great Magickal Retirement on the Hudson River, but he always refused to endorse any theory of what they meant beyond linking them to his unconscious. As he said in his *Confessions*: 'I refuse to assert any theory of what this really means. All memory is a re-awakening of ancient impressions. What I was really doing was penetrating to the deeper layers of my unconscious self'.

So with that in mind, learn that in some sense he had been: the Egyptian priest Ankh-f-n-Khonsu, a Grecian sacred whore named Astarte, the rascally but psychically gifted Edward Kelly, Cagliostro, and the French magus Eliphas Levi.

Violet Firth, right from the start, from her earliest memories as a four-year-old girl, knew that her roots were in lost Atlantis. Later on, as Dion Fortune, she seems to have recovered Egyptian, Nordic, and Cathar past lives, but was certain that her immediate incarnation prior to this one had been as a pirate in the Spanish Main, who had been hanged in Bristol.

Yet neither of them were obsessed by this aspect of their magical and magickal memory at all.

Since their deaths, however, a number of men have claimed to have been reincarnations of Crowley, though none of them had one-tenth of 1 percent of his genius, and a couple were just mentally ill. Likewise, I personally have met a number of earnest and thoroughly delightful souls who have felt that they were reincarnations of Dion Fortune—women with real gifts on magical levels, but who were unable to answer hard questions about her life and got rather annoyed that I wouldn't—couldn't—recognise them. In fact, if anyone reading this believes that she is Dion Fortune reborn, then please write and tell me exactly—exactly, mind you—where Violet Firth went to school between the ages of five and eleven.

Personally I rather like the notion of Timothy Leary who, after some heavy acid tripping at Bou Saada with Brian Barritt, started to think of himself as a 'continuation' of Crowley, as opposed to a reincarnation as it is normally understood. To him there were strong parallels between his and Barritt's experiences, and those of Dee and Kelly, and by extension Crowley and Neuberg. Leary saw himself as part of a line of sorcerers who recurred throughout history, and felt that he was playing out a kind of cosmic script for a regular transformative current that repeated itself throughout time.[1]

So in this sense Dion Fortune may well have been playing out a cosmic script in which she continued the magic of Morgana le Fay, and before that of a Priestess of Isis, and long long before any of them, of a Sea Priestess from Atlantis.

And so we may well find ourselves involved in this same holographic script, continuing the roles of the Logos of the Aeon and the Shakti of the Age, helping manifest this transformative current—

---

1. See John Higgs, *I Have America Surrounded: The Life of Timothy Leary* (Fort Lee, NJ: Barricade Books, 2006).

whether it is called the Aeon of Horus, Maat, or simply the Aquarian Age.

Gods bless us every one . . .

AFTERWORD

This has just been something of an overview of two extraordinary people who need and deserve more than a few thumbnail sketches to be appreciated. There are vast amounts of information on both souls on the World Wide Web, which as far as am I concerned is a lower analogue of the Halls of Akasha—but far easier to access. In fact, Dion Fortune and Aleister Crowley are like the icons on a computer screen: click on them and astonishing things can open up. It simply requires individual effort. Websites you may start with are:

www.oto.org
www.sria.org
www.angelfire.com/az/garethknight/
www.cornelius93.com/
www.servantsofthelight.org
www.alric.pwp.blueyonder.co.uk

For further reading of actual books, I would suggest . . .
The best biography on Crowley is Lawrence Sutin's *Do What Thou Wilt*. Although he is not a magician, Sutin manages to show a great insight and certain degree of sympathy for the ramifications and subtleties of the magickal path. Also, John Symond's *The Great Beast* is

still compulsive reading, although hardened Thelemites seem never to forgive him for not accepting the *Book of the Law*, and (deservedly) showing Crowley's very worst sides. In this respect, Snoo Wilson's extraordinary novel I, *Crowley* is a brilliant evocation of the man himself. And of course there is the majestic *Confessions*, wherein the Great Beast tells his own story in his own inimitable words. The latter two books by the Beast can be tracked down and read online at various sites. There is also the very curious *Aleister Crowley and the Ouija Board* by J. Edward Cornelius, which points out some unusual aspects to the Old Master, and the impressively researched *Secret Agent 666* by Richard B. Spence, which should be compulsory reading for all those intrigued by this field.

Although my own *Priestess: The Life and Magic of Dion Fortune* was the first general biography of that woman, and has been recently expanded and updated with more emphasis on her family and background, I see it as something of an outer court to Gareth Knight's *Dion Fortune and the Inner Light*, which was written with full and envious access to the archives of the Society of the Inner Light. There is also *The Quest for Dion Fortune* by Janine Chapman, and *The Story of Dion Fortune* by Charles Fielding and Carr Collins. To read Dion's own words on her own life, the classic *Psychic Self-Defence* is a must, and one of the most extraordinary books ever written.

On a personal note, do I accept Thelema? No, although as a young man I would quote 'Do What Thou Wilt' whenever I wanted to get my own way and not feel guilty about things. But as someone who has worked with the equal and balancing energies of Horus and Set for an exceedingly long time now, I rather agree with Jean Overton Fuller that *Liber AL* is an insult to Horus, and hence, I would add, a malignment of Set also. Perdurabo creaked open the door of his soul to let the Horus-light of the Aeon shine through him, but the rest of his quirks and peccadilloes rather sullied it. The older I get, the more

I think he didn't really understand the Egyptian deities he invoked so often, although he made all the loud noises and got suitably hammered by them at times.

Do I accept *The Cosmic Doctrine*? No. Quite simply I don't understand a word of it. If it is relevant today, and capable of changing lives, I can't see how. At least the *Book of the Law* has some lines of beautiful prose, and spark enough to give a young man or woman some fire in the blood. But I do accept DF's own dictum: I *desire to Know, in order to Serve*. If magick isn't for the common weal, what good is it?

Had we been contemporaries, would I have invited Crowley around to tea? No, but I would have been delighted to meet him on neutral ground, after making sure that my wife, my daughters, and my money were safely out of reach. And Dion Fortune? Yes. She could come to my house anytime. I'd trust her with my soul.

Who was the better writer? Dion Fortune. Too many people mistake Crowley's obscurity with profundity, and his heroin-befuddled scholarship with wisdom. Most people are afraid to challenge his correspondences, for example, under the apparent belief that he was omniscient, or because they are too lazy or too reluctant to do original work of the sort of which the Master Therion himself would have approved.

All things considered, whose life would I rather have lived? Without a doubt Crowley's—though without the buggery and the Cakes of Light. I think Cyril Connolly's perception that Aleister Crowley was the man who bridged the gap between Oscar Wilde and Hitler was not without a keen edge of truth. There is a sense in which every perceived fault and failure of the present era can be seen as manifested in Crowley a century ahead of its time: the overwhelming and omnipresent drug abuse, the hedonism, the lack of parental responsibility, creating feral children, the obsession with darkness and the need to appal, the constant borrowing without any possibility of repayment, the megalomania, the lack of generosity, the urge to destroy via 'shock and awe' in the belief that it will set free ... Yet I still admire him.

In sharp contrast, in terms of simple human adventure and excitement, Dion Fortune doesn't seem to have lived much at all.

Do I believe that people have linked with them psychically after their deaths? Yes, I have to. An energy or node of consciousness which took the form of Dion Fortune was in my head for many years, and caused many things to happen in the outer realm. Similarly, an energy or node of consciousness which took the form of Ankh-f-n-Khonsu spent some time in the heads of both myself and the late, great Billie Walker-John when we were writing our *Inner Guide to Egypt*.

Do I believe that Dion accepted the Law of Thelema and would have turned her group over to the stewardship of Crowley had she lived? Not exactly. I believe that in broad general terms she would have conceded that 'Do What Thou Wilt' was a necessary antidote to the suffocating strictures of the time, but that the complete acceptance of *Liber* AL would have seemed as unnecessary and unpalatable to her as acceptance of *The Cosmic Doctrine* would be for me.

Yet others are convinced that Crowley spoke the truth and that she did indeed accept the Law in its purest form, but kept very secret about it. If that were truly the case, then perhaps my deliciously silly daydream of the present-day heads of the Typhonian and Caliphate versions of the O. T. O. turning up at the headquarters of the Society of the Inner Light in London and asking to be made at home might one day come true.[1]

Whatever the truth behind Aleister Crowley and Dion Fortune as representatives of the Logos of the Aeon and the Shakti of the Age, they are perhaps best thought of as representing energies, examples, and potentials within each of us. We can reach out to them if we will, knowing that we are actually reaching toward aspects of our inner

---

1. Kenneth Grant and William Breeze, respectively.

selves. We might make absolute idiots of ourselves in the process, but at least we will be taking the first steps toward the light, creating interesting shadows behind, and trying to fulfil our potential in ways that would have made the historical figures right proud.

APPENDIX A

This brilliant chart by Jerry E. Cornelius, a tireless collector and interpreter of all things Crowleyan, shows exactly how much Gerald Gardner took from existing writings of the Great Beast in order to create his own religion of Wicca:

Aleister Crowley (or channelled through him)	Gerald Gardner
Liber LX (Gnostic Mass) Part IV OF THE CEREMONY OF THE OPENING OF THE VEIL (1913) '... the understanding dark, not unto Thee may we attain, unless Thine image be Love. Therefore by seed and root and stem and bud and leaf and flower and fruit do we invoke Thee'.	**Drawing Down the Moon (1949)** 'I Invoke and beseech Thee, O mighty Mother of all life and fertility. By seed and root, by stem and bud, by leaf and flower and fruit, by Life and Love, do I invoke Thee to descend into the body of thy servant and High Priestess [name]'.

Liber AL (Book of the Law) Chap. I (1904)	'Lift Up the Veil' (1949)
verse 58. 'I give unimaginable joys on earth: certainty, not faith, while in life, upon death; peace unutterable, rest, ecstasy; nor do I demand aught in sacrifice'.	'... Let ecstasy be mine, and joy on earth even to me, To Me, For I am a gracious Goddess. I give unimaginable joys on earth, certainty, not faith, while in life! And upon death, peace unutterable, rest, and ecstasy, nor do I demand aught in sacrifice'.
verse 61. 'But to love me is better than all things: if under the night stars in the desert thou presently burnest mine incense before me, invoking me with a pure heart, and the Serpent flame therein, thou shalt come a little to lie in my bosom. For one kiss wilt thou then be willing to give all; but whoso gives one particle of dust shall lose all in that hour. Ye shall gather goods and store of women and spices; ye shall wear rich jewels; ye shall exceed the nations of the earth in spendour & pride; but always in the love of me, and so shall ye come to my joy. I charge you earnestly to come before me in a single robe, and covered with a rich headdress. I love you! I yearn to you! Pale or purple, veiled or voluptuous, I who am all pleasure and purple, and drunkenness of the innermost sense, desire you. Put on the wings, and arouse the coiled splendour within you: come unto me!'	'... I love you: I yearn for you: pale or purple, veiled or voluptuous. I who am all pleasure, and purple and drunkenness of the innermost senses, desire you. Put on the wings, arouse the coiled splendor within you. Come unto me,

Chapter II verse 6. 'I am the flame that burns in every heart of man, and in the core of every star. I am Life, and the giver of Life, yet therefore is the knowledge of me the knowledge of death'.	'for I am the flame that burns in the heart of every man, and the core of every Star'
verses 35 & 42. 'Let the rituals be rightly performed with joy & beauty! A feast every day in your hearts in the joy of my rapture!'	'... Let it be your inmost divine self who art lost in the constant rapture of infinite joy. Let the rituals be rightly performed with joy and beauty. Remember that all acts of love and pleasure are my rituals'
verse 20. 'Beauty and strength, leaping laughter and delicious languor, force and fire, are of us'.	'... So let there be beauty and strength, leaping laughter, force and fire by within you. And if thou sayest, "I have journeyed unto thee, and it availed me not", rather shalt thou say, "I called upon thee, and I waited patiently, and Lo, thou wast with me from the beginning", for they that ever desired me shall ever attain me, even to the end of all desire'.
O. T. O. Degree Initiations I, II, & III (Original, circa the 1920s)	**Wiccan Degree Initiations I, II, & III** (Original 1949)
Liber LX (Gnostic Mass) Part IV OF THE CEREMONY OF THE OPENING OF THE VEIL (1913) 'Thee therefore whom we adore we also invoke. By the power of the lifted Lance!'	**III Degree Initiation (1949)** 'Therefore, whom we adore, we also invoke, by the power of the lifted lance.

'O circle of Stars whereof our Father is but the younger brother, marvel beyond imagination, soul of infinite space, before whom Time is Ashamed, the mind bewildered, and the understanding dark, not unto Thee may we attain, unless Thine image be Love. Therefore by seed and root and stem and bud and leaf and flower and fruit do we invoke Thee'.

'O circle of stars [kiss], whereof our Father is but the younger brother [kiss], Marvel beyond imagination, soul of infinite space, before whom time is ashamed, the mind bewildered and understanding dark, not unto thee may we attain unless thine image be of love [kiss]. Therefore, by seed and root, and stem and bud and leaf and flower and fruit do we invoke thee,

Liber AL (Book of the Law) Chap.I
(1904)
verse 27.

'Then the priest answered & said unto the Queen of Space, kissing her lovely brows, and the dew of her light bathing his whole body in a sweet-smelling perfume of sweat: O Nuit, continuous one of Heaven, let it be ever thus; that men speak not of Thee as One but as None; and let them speak not of thee at all, since thou art continuous!'

"O, Queen of space, O dew of light, O continuous one of the Heavens [kiss]. Let it be ever thus, that men speak not of Thee as one, but as none, and let them not speak of thee at all, since thou art continuous,

verse 60.

'My number is 11, as all their numbers who are of us. The Five Pointed Star, with a Circle in the Middle, & the circle is Red. My colour is black to the blind, but the blue & gold are seen of the seeing. Also I have a secret glory for them that love me'.

"for thou art the point within the circle [kiss], which we adore [kiss], the fount of life without which we would not be [kiss]. And in this way truly are erected the Holy Twin Pillars Boaz and Joachim [kisses breasts]. In beauty and strength were they erected, to the wonder and glory of all men." (Eightfold Kiss: 3 points, Lips, 2 Breasts and back to lips; 5 points)

'Liber LX (Gnostic Mass) Part IV OF
THE CEREMONY OF THE OPENING
OF THE VEIL (1913)

'O secret of secrets that art hidden in
the being of all that lives, not Thee do
we adore, for that which adoreth is also
Thou. Thou art That, and That am I'.

'O Secrets of secrets that art hidden
in the being of all lives. Not thee do
we adore, for that which adoreth is
also thou. Thou art that and That am
I [kiss].

Liber AL (Book of the Law) Chap.II
(1904)
verse 6.

'I am the flame that burns in every heart
of man, and in the core of every star. I
am Life, and the giver of Life, yet
therefore is the knowledge of me the
knowledge of death'.

'I am the flame that burns in every
man, and in the core of every star
[kiss]. I am Life and the giver of Life,
yet therefore is the knowledge of me
the Knowledge of Death [kiss].

verse 23.

'I am alone: there is no God where I am'.

'I am alone, the Lord within ourselves
whose name is Mystery of Mysteries
[kiss].

Liber LX (Gnostic Mass) Part IV OF
THE CEREMONY OF THE OPENING
OF THE VEIL (1913)

'Thou that art One, our Lord in the
Universe the Sun, our Lord in ourselves
whose name is Mystery of Mystery,
uttermost being whose radiance
enlightening the worlds is also the
breath that maketh every God even and
Death to tremble before Thee-By the
Sign of Light + appear Thou glorious
upon the throne of the Sun.

'Make open the path of intelligence
between us. For these truly are the 5
points of fellowship [on the right appears an illuminated diagram of the
point-up triangle above the pentacle,
the symbol for the third degree], feet
to feet, knee to knee, groin to groin,
breast to breast, arms around back,
lips to lips, by the Great and Holy
Names Abracadabra, Aradia, and Cer-
nunnos. Magus and High Priestess:

'Make open the path of creation and of intelligence between us and our minds. Enlighten our understanding.

'Encourage our hearts. Let thy light crystallize itself in our blood, fulfilling us of Resurrection'.

'Encourage our hearts, Let thy Light crystallize itself in our blood, fulfilling us of Resurrection

Liber LX (Gnostic Mass) Part VIII OF THE MYSTIC MARRIAGE AND CONSUMMATION OF THE ELE-MENTS (1913)

'There is no part of me that is not of the Gods'.

'for there is no part of us that is not of the Gods'.

Liber AL (Book of the Law) Chap.II (1904)

The Sabbat Rituals (1949)
November Eve

verse 6.
'I am the flame that burns in every heart of man, and in the core of every star. I am Life, and the giver of Life, yet therefore is the knowledge of me the knowledge of death'.

'Dread Lord of the shadows, god of life and the giver of life. Yet is the knowledge of thee the knowledge of death. Open wide, I pray thee, thy gates through which all must pass'.

Liber LX (Gnostic Mass) Part IV OF THE CEREMONY OF THE OPENING OF THE VEIL (1913)

February Eve

'Thou that art One, our Lord in the Universe the Sun, our Lord in ourselves whose name is Mystery of Mystery, uttermost being whose radiance enlightening the worlds is also the breath that maketh every God even and Death to tremble before Thee-By the

'Dread Lord of death and Resurrec-tion, life and the giver of life, Lord within ourselves, whose name is Mystery of Mysteries, encourage our hearts. Let the light crystalize in our blood, fulfilling us of resurrection, for there is no part of us that is not of the

'Sign of Light + appear Thou glorious upon the throne of the Sun.

'Make open the path of creation and of intelligence between us and our minds Enlighten our understanding.

'Encourage our hearts. Let thy light crystallize itself in our blood, fulfilling us of Resurrection'.

'the understanding dark, not unto Thee may we attain, unless Thine image be Love. Therefore by seed and root and stem and bud and leaf and flower and fruit do we invoke Thee'.

Liber AL (Book of the Law) Chap.I
(1904) verse 13.

'I am above you and in you. My ecstasy is in yours. My joy is to see your joy'.

verse 53.
'This shall regenerate the world, the little world my sister, my heart & my tongue, unto whom I send this kiss. Also, o scribe and prophet, though thou be of the princes, it shall not assuage thee nor absolve thee. But ecstasy be

gods. Descend, we pray thee, upon this thy servant and Priest (name)'.

May Eve

'I invoke thee and call upon thee, O mighty Mother of us all, bringer of all fruitfulness, By seed and root, by stem and bud, by leaf and flower and fruit, by life and love, do we invoke thee, to descend upon the body of thy servant and Priestess here'.

To Help the Sick (1953)

'Ever remember the promise of the goddess, "For ecstasy is mine and joy on earth" so let there ever be joy in your heart. Greet people with joy, be glad to see them. If times be hard, think, "It might have been worse. I at least have known the joys of the Sabbath, and I will know them again"'.

'thine and joy of earth: ever To me! To me!'

Verse 58.
'I give unimaginable joys on earth: certainty, not faith, while in life, upon death; peace unutterable, rest, ecstasy; nor do I demand aught in sacrifice'.

'But keep your own mind happy. Remember the Words of the Goddess: "I give unimaginable joys on Earth, certainty, not faith, while in life, and upon death, peace unutterable, rest, and ecstasy, and the promise that you will return again". In the old days many of us went to the flames laughing and singing, and so we may again. We may have joy in life and beauty, and peace and Death and the promise of return'.

The 93 Current

Do what thou wilt shall be the whole of the Law. Love is the law, love under will.

The Wiccan Rede

Bide thy Wiccan law ye must,
In perfect love and perfect trust.
Eight words of Wiccan rede fulfill
'An ye harm none do what ye will'.
Lest in thyself defense it be,
Ever mind the rule of three.
Follow this with mind and heart
Merry we meet, and merry we part.

APPENDIX B

When William G. Gray agreed to let me work on his biography, tinkering with his original manuscript in a way that wouldn't get him sued for libel by just about every magician of the late twentieth century, he felt it was important to pass on this analysis of Crowley, whom he had known as a young boy. I give the contents verbatim, and would no more tinker with his letters now than I would alter the *Book of the Law*. I could handle Crowley in my head, but Bill Gray is a mage too far . . .

14 Bennington St.,
CHELTENHAM
GL50 4ED
24th June 1988

Dear Alan

Thanks for yours which totally ignored the one question I'd asked you, which was specifically if you thought I ought to write up my American experiences for the autobiography. I'd be glad if you'd answer that even if you don't say another word.

So far as <u>your</u> queries are concerned, my official reply is sure, go ahead, and deal with this as you see fit and as you see the subjects you deal with. The important thing is that you see the personalities of the people you're dealing with, and the work they did, as distinct and different topics, however closely they may be connected. For instance, when dealing with Crowley, you cannot overstress the importance of the incident of his mother catching him in bed with the servant girl, and her subsequent treatment of this, because that single occasion determined all the rest of his life and behaviour. If you don't know it, this is what happened.

As you may know, Crowley was brought up by hopelessly narrow-minded relatives of the Strict Plymouth Brethren persuasion. His father died when he was eight, and his mother went to live with an uncle nearly as narrow. Crowley was given no <u>personal</u> love at all, and was a naturally affectionate child with no means of expressing his emotions. When he came to sexual maturity his anxieties and suppressed feelings were beyond description. Apparently he had come to an understanding with the youngish 'maid of all work' as they used to call them, that if ever an opportunity occurred, she would initiate him into the delights of sexual experience. The uncle was apparently absent at the time, and one evening Mrs Crowley announced that she would be attending a religious meeting somewhere, and would not be back until very late. That provided the opportunity needed, and so after a decent interval, young Master Aleister and the girl, who was probably in her late twenties or so, decided to get together. They unwisely but understandably chose Mrs Crowley's big bed to perform in, and indulged in considerable foreplay first. Eventually they got into the bed and commenced the serious business. Suddenly, in virtual mid-bounce, the bedroom door opened and in came Mrs Crowley. The meeting had been cancelled at short notice, and she had come straight home. But as Victorian authors used to say, I will NOT draw a veil over this painful scene. After her first horrified gasp, Mrs C ordered immediate cessation of such a shocking performance. The maid was sacked immediately and dismissed with no wages due, (they could do that in those days) and given an hour to pack her things and depart, but here comes the horrifying part. Mrs Crowley did NOT lose her temper, rage, or otherwise emotionalise. It would have been a lot better if she had, but she didn't. Instead she took the line of what had she ever done to offend God so much that he had sent her such a wicked, wicked, WICKED, WICKED son? She went on and on, lecturing young Aleister concerning his sinful and evil act. I was told that this went on for four hours, with the wretched youth forced to listen to every word and say nothing in his defence. She continued vilifying him in that cold hard voice with every appropriate scriptural quote she could think of, especially from Revelations, particularly mentioning the Great Beast and the Scarlet Woman. In the end, young Aleister was told to spend the rest of the night on his knees praying for forgiveness, and sent away with no supper.

At least that is the story I had from my mother who had it from Victor Newberg [sic], who presumably had it from Crowley himself. I feel that this totally explains Crowley, but whose was the greater sin, his for following a natural instinct, or his mothers for following an unnatural and cruel doctrine, I wouldn't presume to judge. Do bear in mind that poor Aleister hadn't even had an orgasm for this unusual but literal coitus interruptus. Now is it any wonder that he had an odd life? All my own mother did was to warn me about venereal diseases I could catch if I wasn't careful, and advise me on essential points of hygiene. I doubt if there are many mothers today who would act like Mrs Crowley, though there could be some left I suppose.

Bobbie has to go into hospital next week for a small operation on her lower jaw, but so far as I know she will be out in a few days with an aching face plus a disturbed temper. That leaves me here to look after the cats on my own. Now can you tell me whether you think my American story would help my story as it stands/ All I need is a yes or no. Is that too much to ask?

By the way Sphere Books (a branch of Penguins) have just published something by one Anthony Harris, claiming that Jesus was really a <u>woman</u> named Yeshu. He skates around all the awkward points like the circumcision, Jewish ritual baths, the fact that the Romans crucified their condemned <u>naked</u>, and suchlike things, but burbles on about Mary Magdalene, the Cathars, Templars, (whose mysterious 'head' he claims was that of Yeshu herself), the Holy Shroud, and indeed God alone knows what else. I would class this with the 'Manna Machine' and 'Sun Gods in Exile' for pure spoof value. Oh well. If <u>that</u> is publishable, anything is . . . .

Now God Bless and K[eep] Q[uesting]

Bill

SELECTED BIBLIOGRAPHY

By and about Aleister Crowley:

Cornelius, J. Edward. *Aleister Crowley and the Ouija Board*. Port Townsend, WA: Feral House, 2005.

Crowley, Aleister. *777 and Other Qabalistic Writings of Aleister Crowley*. Edited, with an introduction by Israel Regardie. York Beach, ME: Weiser, 1993.

———. *The Confessions of Aleister Crowley*. Edited by John Symonds and Kenneth Grant. London: Jonathan Cape, 1969.

———. *Moonchild*. York Beach, ME: Weiser, 1992.

Crowley, Aleister, with Mary Desti and Leila Waddell. *Magick*. Book 4, parts I–IV. York Beach, ME: Weiser, 1997.

Grant, Kenneth. *Aleister Crowley & The Hidden God*. London: Muller, 1973.

———. *Remembering Aleister Crowley*. London: Skoob, 1991.

Regardie, Israel. *The Eye in the Triangle: An Interpretation of Aleister Crowley*. Phoenix, AZ: Falcon Press, 1993.

Spence, Richard B. *Secret Agent 666: Aleister Crowley, British Intelligence and the Occult*. Port Townsend, WA: Feral House, 2008.

Sutin, Lawrence. *Do What Thou Wilt: A Life of Aleister Crowley*. New York: St. Martin's, 2000.

Symonds, John. *The Great Beast*. London: Mayflower, 1973.

Wilson, Snoo. *I, Crowley: Almost the Last Confession of the Beast*. Oxford: Mandrake, 1997.

By and about Dion Fortune:

Chapman, Janine. *The Quest for Dion Fortune*. York Beach, ME: Weiser, 1993.

Fielding, Charles, and Carr Collins. *The Story of Dion Fortune*. Loughborough, UK: Thoth Publications, 1998.

Fortune, Dion. *Moon Magic*. York Beach, ME: Weiser, 2003.

————. *The Mystical Qabalah*. London: Williams and Norgate, 1935.

————. *Psychic Self-Defence*. York Beach, ME: Weiser, 2001.

————. *The Sea Priestess*. York Beach, ME: Weiser 2003.

Knight, Gareth. *Dion Fortune and the Inner Light*. Loughborough, UK: Thoth Publications, 2000.

Richardson, Alan. *Priestess: The Life and Magic of Dion Fortune* (new and revised edition). Loughborough, UK: Thoth Publications, 2007.

Richardson, Alan, and Marcus Claridge. *The Old Sod: The Odd Life and Inner Work of William G. Gray*. London: Ignotus Press, 2003.

General:

Colquhoun, Ithell. *The Sword of Wisdom*. London: Neville Spearman, 1975.

Gilbert, R. A. *The Golden Dawn Companion*. London: Aquarian Press, 1986.

King, Francis. *Ritual Magic in England*. London: Neville Spearman, 1970.

To Write to the Author

If you wish to contact the author or would like more information about this book, please write to the author in care of Llewellyn Worldwide and we will forward your request. Both the author and publisher appreciate hearing from you and learning of your enjoyment of this book and how it has helped you. Llewellyn Worldwide cannot guarantee that every letter written to the author can be answered, but all will be forwarded. Please write to:

Alan Richardson
℅ Llewellyn Worldwide
2143 Wooddale Drive, Dept. 978-0-7387-1580-3
Woodbury, MN 55125-2989, U.S.A.

Please enclose a self-addressed stamped envelope for reply,
or $1.00 to cover costs. If outside the U.S.A., enclose
an international postal reply coupon.

Many of Llewellyn's authors have websites with additional information and resources. For more information, please visit our website at http://www.llewellyn.com.